Gooseberry Patch Co. ®

A Country Store In Your Mailbox®

Backyard Gatherings

A Country Store In Your Mailbox®

Gooseberry Patch
149 Johnson Drive
Department BOOK
Delaware, OH 43015
★
1·800·85·GOOSE
1-800·854·6673

Copyright 1997, Gooseberry Patch 1-888052-25-2
Fifth Printing, March, 1999

How To Subscribe

Would you like to receive
"A Country Store in Your Mailbox"®?
For a 2-year subscription to our 88-page
Gooseberry Patch catalog, simply send $3.00 to:

Gooseberry Patch
149 Johnson Drive
Department BOOK
Delaware, OH 43015

Contents

DEDICATION

To all our friends who have
ever found delight in twinkling
fireflies, freshly mown clover, and the
laughter of children.

APPRECIATION

A heartfelt thanks to everyone in our Gooseberry
Patch family who share their kind words
and good wishes with us every day.
May your garden be full of happiness!

Join us for a
Country
Weekend

Breakfast & Brunch

Blueberry & Cheese Streusel

This streusel looks elegant, and it's so easy to prepare.

Batter:

2-1/3 c. all-purpose flour
1-1/3 c. sugar
1 t. salt
3/4 c. butter
2 t. baking powder

3/4 c. milk
2 eggs
1 t. vanilla
1 c. fresh blueberries

Filling:

1 c. ricotta cheese
1 egg

2 T. sugar
1 T. lemon peel, grated

Topping:

1/2 c. nuts, chopped
1/3 c. brown sugar

1 t. cinnamon

Prepare batter by combining flour, sugar and salt in a large mixing bowl; using a pastry cutter or 2 knives, cut in butter. Set aside one cup of crumb mixture. To remaining mixture, add baking powder, milk, eggs and vanilla. Beat for 2 minutes then pour mixture into a lightly oiled 13"x9"x2" baking pan; layer blueberries over batter. Combine filling ingredients and layer on top of blueberries. Combine topping ingredients and mix with reserved crumb mixture, sprinkle over filling layer. Bake streusel at 350 degrees for 50 minutes or until toothpick inserted in center comes out clean. Makes 20 servings.

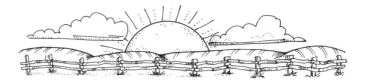

Stuffed French Toast

Take advantage of the fresh supply of June berries!

Filling:

4 oz. cream cheese
4 T. strawberry yogurt
1 T. powdered sugar

2 T. milk
1 c. strawberries, sliced

Toast:

4 large eggs
1 c. milk
2 T. sugar
1/2 t. ground nutmeg

2 to 4 T. butter
8 slices bread
fresh strawberries for garnish

Prepare filling by combining cream cheese, yogurt and powdered sugar until smooth. Add milk until mixture is spreadable. Fold in strawberries and set aside. Using a large mixing bowl, whisk eggs, milk, sugar and nutmeg until thoroughly blended. Over medium heat, melt butter in a non-stick pan. Remove bread slices from egg mixture and place in skillet, cooking both sides until golden. Spread filling mixture on 4 slices of toast, cover with remaining 4 slices. Dust with powdered sugar and garnish with fresh strawberry slices.

Strawberry plants spread quickly! Share some plants with a neighbor or friend along with your favorite jam recipes!

Breakfast & Brunch

Rosemary-Lemon Scones

Wonderful served warm with butter and jam.

2 c. all-purpose flour
2 T. sugar
1 T. baking powder
2 t. fresh rosemary
2 t. lemon peel, grated

1/4 t. salt
1/4 c. butter
2 large eggs, beaten
1/2 c. whipping cream
1 t. cinnamon

Combine flour, sugar, baking powder, rosemary, lemon peel and salt. Using a pastry cutter, cut in butter until mixture resembles crumbs, set aside. In a medium bowl, combine eggs with whipping cream, add to flour mixture and stir well. Dough should be sticky. On a well-floured board, knead dough gently 10 times then shape into an 8-inch circle about one inch in thickness. Cut circle into equal wedges and place on a lightly oiled baking sheet. Sprinkle cinnamon over scones and bake at 400 degrees for 15 minutes or until golden.

For a pretty table accent, tuck cheery red potted geraniums in lunch-size paper bags.

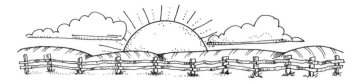

Ham & Asparagus Rolls

Fresh, tender asparagus from your garden makes this a wonderful springtime dish.

1 lb. asparagus, trimmed
brown mustard
16 slices ham
6 T. butter
6 T. all-purpose flour

2 c. milk
salt and pepper
6 oz. Colby cheese, shredded
8 green onions, thinly sliced

Steam asparagus until tender, set aside. Spread mustard on each slice of ham and roll around 2 asparagus spears. Place rolls in an 11"x 8-1/2" baking dish and set aside. Over medium heat, melt butter then blend in flour to form a roux. Stir milk in slowly, add salt and pepper, cheese and onions. Pour over asparagus rolls, cover with foil and bake at 350 degrees for 25 minutes. Makes 8 servings.

The greener your asparagus is, the more tender it will be.

9

Breakfast & Brunch

Savory Cheddar Bake

If you're short on time, this dish is perfect!

1 lb. bulk sausage
1 red pepper, diced
1 green pepper, diced
1 medium onion, diced
2 c. Cheddar cheese, grated

6 eggs
1/4 c. milk
1/2 t. garlic powder
1 t. pepper

Crumble sausage in a saucepan, cook thoroughly; drain. Sauté peppers and onion until tender. Place sausage on the bottom of a lightly oiled 1-1/2 quart casserole dish; lightly pressing into place, layer vegetables and cheese on top. In a small bowl, combine eggs, milk, garlic powder and pepper. Pour egg mixture over vegetables and bake at 350 degrees for 30 minutes. Cool slightly, cut into wedges. Serves 6.

For a pretty brunch table setting, lay a red and white quilt on your breakfast table. Fill a watering can with ivy and tie a cheery red gingham bow to the handle. Serve breakfast on old-fashioned spatterware plates.

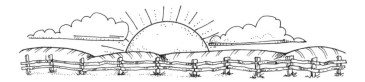

Garden-Fresh Frittata

Pick vegetables fresh from your garden for this delicious meal!

3 egg whites
1 egg
2 T. chives, chopped
1/8 t. salt
1/8 t. pepper
1/2 c. new potatoes, cubed
1/2 c. broccoli flowerets

1/4 c. sweet yellow pepper, chopped
1/3 c. water
1/2 t. canola oil
Garnish: chives, tomatoes, Cheddar cheese

Beat together egg whites, egg, chives, salt and pepper until thoroughly combined; set aside. Lightly coat an oven-proof skillet with vegetable cooking spray, add potatoes and sauté until browned. Add broccoli, yellow pepper and water, cover skillet with lid. Continue to cook until potatoes are tender, remove cover and allow liquid to evaporate. Add oil to skillet thoroughly coating all vegetables, pour egg mixture over vegetables, allow to set slightly, then stir. Cover skillet and cook frittata until eggs are set, but not dry. Remove lid from skillet and place skillet under broiler allowing the top to brown. Garnish with chives, diced tomatoes and grated cheese if desired.

Breakfast & Brunch

Pesto & Scallion Omelete

Preserve the fresh herb flavors of summer...make your own pesto sauce, it's easy!

2 T. butter
2 T. canola oil
6 eggs
salt and pepper
2 T. water

1/4 c. scallions, chopped
1/4 c. pesto sauce
Garnish: garlic chives, cherry
    tomatoes, parsley

Melt butter and oil in an 8-inch skillet coating sides and bottom well. Separate eggs into 2 small mixing bowls. Beat whites until they form soft peaks; beat yolks until frothy. Add salt, pepper and water to yolks blending well; blend in whites, add scallions. Pour mixture into hot skillet and allow edges to set. Gently lift edges allowing center of omelette to run underneath. When eggs are set, spoon pesto sauce on top and fold. Garnish as desired.

Pesto Sauce:

2 c. fresh basil, washed and
    dried
3 cloves garlic

4 T. walnuts
1/2 c. olive oil
1/2 c. Parmesan cheese, grated

Place basil, garlic, walnuts and oil in food processor until mixture forms a paste; add cheese and blend. Remove from processor and blend again with a spoon.

Serve individual-size omeletes...pour your ingredients into lightly-oiled muffin tins and bake as usual.

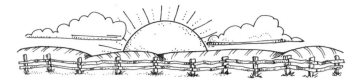

Homemade Poppy Seed Dressing

This fresh and tangy dressing will really dress up your fruit. Try it over kiwi, strawberries and mandarin orange slices.

3/4 c. sugar
1-1/2 t. onion salt
1 t. dry mustard

1/3 c. white vinegar
1 c. vegetable oil
1 T. poppy seeds

Combine sugar, onion salt and dry mustard mixing until well-blended. Add vinegar, mixing well; then gradually add vegetable oil. Beat at medium speed until dressing thickens, stir in poppy seeds. Pour into a decorative glass bottle, cover and refrigerate. Makes 1-1/2 cups of dressing.

Serve your poppy seed dressing in old-fashioned milk bottles...charming!

Breakfast & Brunch

Refreshing Citrus Blush

The combination of these fruits will tingle your tongue!

4 ruby red grapefruit, halved
3 tangerines, halved

1 mango, peeled and chopped
1 T. honey

Using a juicer, squeeze grapefruit and tangerine halves until fruits yield 4 cups of juice; set aside. Place mango chunks and honey in a food processor and pulse until smooth. Add to juices, blend well. Serve chilled.

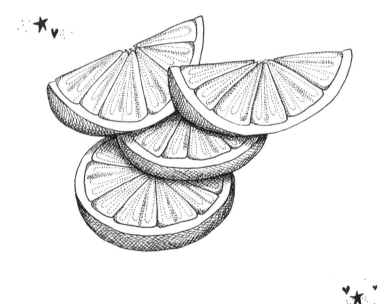

Give a "Special Delivery" breakfast to someone under the weather. Fill a basket with homemade jams, or pancake mix. Tuck in a loaf of warm bread or pound cake made from your favorite recipe. Tie a ribbon around the handle, then visit a special friend!

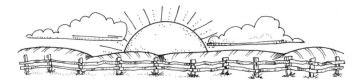

Tomato Cocktail

A great appetizer to serve while you're putting the finishing touches on brunch.

1 qt. 14-oz. can of tomato juice
juice of 1/2 a lemon
1 t. sweet onion, grated

1 t. Worcestershire sauce
1/8 t. hot pepper sauce
celery sticks for garnish

Combine all ingredients together; chill. Serves 6.

The best way to get real enjoyment out of the garden is to put on a wide straw hat, dress in thin loose-fitting clothes, hold a little trowel in one hand and a cool drink in the other, and tell the man where to dig.
-Charles Barr

Breakfast & Brunch

Fresh Melon Sorbet

Light and delicious.

1 medium honeydew, seeded
and pared

1/4 c. sugar
1/4 c. lime juice

Cut honeydew into cubes and purée in a food processor or blender. Place in a large mixing bowl with remaining ingredients. Stir well until sugar is thoroughly dissolved. Spoon into an ice cream maker and freeze according to manufacturer's directions. Serves 6.

Add some pretty lighting to your table! Tuck votives into tart pans, on top of pudding molds, inside graters, or on top of bobbins.

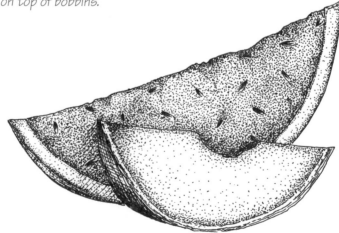

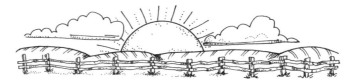

Handmade Invitations

The anticipation begins as soon as your invitations are received! Your guests will want to wake up early and join you for brunch if you make your invitations special!

Paper can be found in a rainbow of colors at any stationery store, along with a wide range of pens, markers and colored pencils. Decorate your invitations with ribbon, appliqués, or pressed flowers. It's also fun to use fruit and vegetable stamps for your invitations. For a garden theme, try dipping half a pepper, radish or lemon into acrylic paint and then firmly pressing it onto paper.

Purchase heavy cardstock and cut invitations into your own special designs; leaves, flowers, or even a rooster to signal it's a special "early-bird" event.

Give as much thought to the wording on your invitation as you do creating it. Clearly name the date, time, place and if any special dress is required. Add an R.S.V.P. to each invitation, but be prepared to telephone guests who do not respond.

Most importantly…be creative and have fun!

Breakfast & Brunch

Create a Welcoming Buffet

Let us share some of our favorite ways to set up a brunch buffet table; they're easy and would make any guest feel special.

Place an old-fashioned coffee grinder, spice box, graniteware coffee pot, or basket of eggs on the table for a casual feel. Cover the table with homespun fabric and use wooden bowls, crocks and baskets as serving dishes.

If you're hosting a special occasion such as a bridal shower, decorate your table with floral-patterned dishes, lace tablecloths and pastel candles. Intertwine ivy along the table and create a centerpiece of pink roses, baby's breath, pansies and violets. Tie wispy bows of tulle and satin ribbon to the table corners and drape the chairs with netting.

A baby shower is another wonderful get-together for family and friends; celebrate with a brunch! Create a centerpiece the mother-to-be can keep. Cover a white-washed grapevine wreath with booties, bottles, pacifier, rattles and teething rings. Tuck in baby's breath and pastel bows…darling! Stack the gifts in an old-fashioned buggy or cradle.

Use the ocean to inspire your buffet. Use vivid colors for your table…red, white, blue and yellow. Add to the atmosphere by using seashells, netting or white roping scattered along the top of the table. Add red votive candles and serve beverages in vivid cobalt blue tumblers.

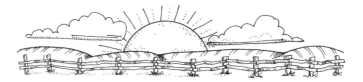

Black-eyed Susan Heartstring

Do you remember making daisy chains as a child? This is a variation of that favorite pastime. String it across your garden gate to welcome friends to your home.

You'll need approximately 50 black-eyed Susans, a thin needle with a large eye and approximately 44 inches of nylon fishing line. Collect your black-eyed Susans and keep them in a tall container of cool water. The petals become delicate after they've been picked, so you'll want to work as quickly as possible. Work with one blossom at a time, leaving the remaining flowers in the water until they're needed.

Thread your needle with the fishing line and tie a loop at one end. Cut the stem off a flower as close to the blossom as possible, and push the needle through the center. Slide the stem to the end of the string and repeat with the remaining flowers.

When you reach the end of your fishing line, remove the needle and tie a second loop for hanging. Your heartstring will stay fresh for one day; or you can let it dry into a pretty summer keepsake.

Earth laughs in flowers.
-Ralph Waldo Emerson

Come into the Garden

Furnish your garden with items that welcome your guests and set the mood for an outdoor gathering.

Pathways through the garden not only allow your guests to wander and enjoy the plants, but can add interest also. Be creative; use stepping stones, cobbles, stone slabs, or brick. Edge your walkway with wonderful flowers that spill over; such as honesty or sweet woodruff. Old millstones make unique steps when paired with a brick path.

An old wooden rain barrel is useful as well as decorative. It looks beautiful surrounded by tall flowers such as hollyhocks or foxgloves, and the rainwater inside will be wonderful for your potted plants.

One of the best things about having a garden is to be able to relax in it and enjoy its beauty. Garden benches can be made from a discarded old church pew, slabs of stone or slate, or strong logs placed in the ground with a simple plank across them.

Adding birdbaths, birdfeeders and sundials also make a garden attractive. Birdbaths of stone or concrete can be made to look old by coating them with sour milk. Add a splash of color to your garden by stacking wooden washtubs or firkins that have been filled with red geraniums.

If your garden gathering is during the day, be sure to provide some shade for your guests. Set up your tables under large, leafy trees or under an umbrella. If the party spills over into evening, provide soft lighting...candles, lanterns, kerosene lamps and luminarias all provide beautiful lighting. Tuck oversize candles into planters and place floating candles in large bowls of water tinted a cool color such as pink or blue.

He who plants a garden,
plants happiness.
—Old Chinese Proverb

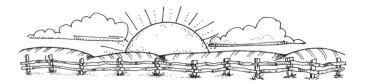

A Springtime Topiary

Dried flowers from your garden make this a long-lasting and lovely table decoration.

30 dried strawflowers
12" straight branch
5" foam ball
3-1/2 oz. green reindeer moss

florist's foam
decorative flowerpot
Spanish moss
36" ribbon

Remove the stems from the straw flowers just below the blossom and set aside. Gently push one end of the branch one inch deep into the foam ball. To keep it secure, remove the branch and coat the end with hot glue, replace the branch in the foam ball; allow to dry.

Apply hot glue to a flat piece of moss and place it on the foam ball; holding it in place briefly until glue sets. Glue a strawflower next to the moss and allow glue to set. In a random pattern, continue alternating moss and strawflowers until foam ball is covered.

Cut florist's foam to fit flowerpot snugly and insert branch in the center of the foam. Use hot glue if necessary to keep the branch secure. After adding enough Spanish moss to cover the top of the foam, complete your topiary by tying a ribbon around the branch.

A wire basket full of brown eggs makes a lovely breakfast centerpiece.

Fruitful Ice Decanter

This is a beautiful table display for a bottle of orange or grapefruit juice. Thoroughly rinse an empty half-gallon milk carton and place 2 inches of water inside. Insert an empty juice bottle in the middle. To anchor the bottle down, cross 2 lengths of florist's tape over the top of the bottle and over the sides of the carton; freeze solid. Remove carton from freezer. Around the outside of the bottle, add a few raspberries, strawberry, lemon, or orange slices, curled lemon or orange peel, variegated mint sprigs, leaves or petals from lemon-scented geraniums. You could even tuck in some rose hips, lilac or dogwood flowers if you like.

To keep the fruit from floating to the top, fill the carton only one-third full with fruit and water; refreeze. This will suspend the fruit and mint sprigs in the decanter. Repeat 2 more times using the same layering and freezing method.

When ready to serve, remove the bottle (pour a little warm water in the bottle if it's difficult to remove) and tear off the paper carton. Insert your full bottle of juice and place your ice decanter on a tray or decorative plate to catch any melting water.

Serve a variety of different cheeses at your brunch...perfect for your guests to nibble on! Line a white-washed basket with red and white homespun, tie a red ticking bow on the handle and fill it with an assortment of cheeses and crackers.

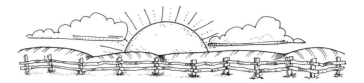

May Day Raspberry Baskets

In Victorian England, May Day was celebrated by secretly leaving a basket of freshly picked flowers on a friend's or neighbor's porch. Imagine what a lovely surprise! This May 1st, begin a new tradition in your family with this easy-to-do garden idea.

Begin by gathering roses and lady's mantle from your garden. Keep them in a cool pail of water so they'll remain fresh.

Cut a block of florist's foam to fit inside your basket, remove and thoroughly soak it water. You may want to insert a plastic liner in your basket first to protect it from water stains, then insert your foam block. Cut short sprays of lady's mantle and place them around the outer edges of the basket, leaving the center open. Tuck in enough lady's mantle to create a full, lush basket, and fill in any spaces to hide the foam block.

Wash and pat dry one pint of raspberries and place them in the middle of your basket over the foam. Mound them up in the center, adding more if necessary. If you'd like, add a raffia bow to the handle...a beautiful, and tasty, May Day gift!

For a casual outdoor gathering, serve brunch on cheery blue and white dishes arranged on yellow and white homespun placemats and tuck a bouquet of sunflowers in an old blue spatterware coffee pot.

Breakfast & Brunch

Birdhouse Swag Holders

Bring a part of the outdoors in! When warm weather arrives replace the heavy logs in your fireplace with a big basket of flowers, add a floral slipcover or some toss pillows to your sofa or favorite chair and open the windows to allow the fresh spring breezes in! Add a touch of charm by creating these Birdhouse Swag Holders; they're so easy!

Purchase 2 birdhouses for each window. Choose colors that compliment your decor or just choose fun, summery birdhouses covered in sunflower or ivy patterns.

Locate and mark the center on each side of the birdhouse. Make an initial hole with a drill, then use a keyhole saw to create a circular opening; repeat on the other side. Make the opening large enough to slip your swag through. Attach the birdhouses at the top corners of your window and slip your swag through as you would through a swag bracket.

If you don't have swags at your windows, choose a length of colorful summer fabric and slip it through the openings. Beautiful!

Place your favorite cut flowers in a vase, then tuck the vase inside a brown paper bag. Hot glue a homespun bow on the corner...a cute centerpiece.

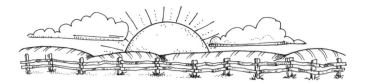

Flower & Fruit Table Ring

A beautiful ring of flowers from your country garden.

scented geranium leaves
lady's mantle
purple coneflowers
roses

1 pt. fresh strawberries
10" florist's foam ring
toothpicks

Keep your flowers fresh by placing them in cool water until ready to use. Thoroughly soak your foam ring in water, remove and place on a circular tray to catch drips.

Cut sprigs of geranium leaves and lady's mantle and arrange them around the ring. Also remember to tuck sprigs inside and along the bottom edge of the ring to hide foam. Add the coneflowers and roses at random along the top and sides of the ring.

Pierce the strawberries with the toothpicks and insert in the foam placing as many as you'd like among the flowers. You may want to keep some extras on hand in case your guests can't resist a nibble! Place the arrangement on your table and spray with cool water to help keep it fresh.

Breakfast & Brunch

A Meadow Garden

What could be lovelier than enjoying brunch where the scent of wild-flowers is as refreshing as a spring breeze? Create your own meadow garden and enjoy their old-fashioned beauty; it's easier than you might think.

After finding the perfect spot for your garden, till the soil to a depth of 8 inches, removing any weeds by hand. To improve the soil, mix in some compost and peat moss then rake the soil to smooth out the seedbed.

Purchase seeds in a variety of old-fashioned favorites such as statice, sweet pea, annual phlox, flax, yarrow, baby's breath, coreopsis, holly-hock, daisy and salvia. Mix the seeds with sand for even distribution and then scatter them sparsely over the soil. Cover with 1/4 inch of soil and water to encourage germination.

Allow the flowers to go to seed in the fall and you'll have even more blooms next year. In no time, you'll have beautiful masses of easy-care flowers.

You can "paint" a face on toast for the kids! Combine one tablespoon of milk and 3 drops of food coloring, "paint" on bread, then pop in the toaster!

Leisurely Lunch
under the trees

Leisurely Lunch

Spiced Lemonade

Serve in icy frosted glasses, with a skewer of fresh fruit.

6 6-inch cinnamon sticks
1 t. ground allspice

2 c. water
1 qt. fresh lemonade

Add cinnamon sticks and allspice to a saucepan, cover with water and simmer 10 minutes; strain. Add mixture to lemonade, stir well and chill.

Stencil or paint flowers on a new garden glove; let dry. Wrap guests' silverware in a cloth napkin and tuck inside the garden glove. Place a glove on each plate...a clever favor for guests to take home!

Turkey-Dijon Super Sub

A complete meal in minutes!

1 loaf sourdough bread, sliced in
   half lengthways
2/3 c. mayonnaise
2 T. Dijon mustard
1 lb. turkey, thinly sliced
12 bacon slices, crisply cooked

1 avocado, sliced
6 tomato slices
6 American cheese slices
1 sweet onion, sliced into rings
1 bell pepper, sliced into rings
shredded lettuce

Combine mayonnaise and mustard in a small bowl, spread half on bottom slice of sourdough bread. Layer remaining ingredients in order, spread remaining mayonnaise mixture on top half of bread. Cover and slice into 6 servings.

*He who shares the joy in what he's grown spreads joy abroad
and doubles his own. -Anonymous*

Leisurely Lunch

Red Potato Salad

An easy, colorful potato salad.

1 lb. red potatoes
16-oz. pkg. frozen mixed
    vegetables
1/3 c. mayonnaise-style salad
    dressing

1/3 c. sour cream
1/2 c. red onion, chopped
1 lb. ham, chopped

Cook potatoes until tender, cool and cut into chunks. Cook frozen vegetables according to the package directions; drain and set aside. In a mixing bowl, combine salad dressing, sour cream and red onion. Stir in potatoes, vegetables and ham. Place in a covered container and refrigerate overnight. Serves 6.

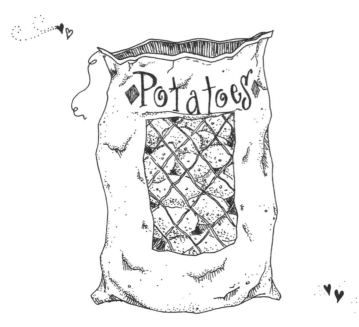

Create a delicate spring centerpiece of purple lilacs, yellow and pink tulips and dogwood branches.

Layered Italian Sandwich

Layers of salami, pepperoni and melted cheese make this a hit at any gathering.

1 lb. frozen bread dough, thawed
1/4 lb. salami, thinly sliced
1/4 lb. genoa ham, thinly sliced
1/4 lb. provolone, thinly sliced

2-oz. pkg. pepperoni slices
8 oz. mushrooms, sliced
1 green pepper, cut into rings

Place dough on a foil lined baking sheet and press into a 13"x10" rectangle. Layer salami, ham, provolone and pepperoni in center of dough, add mushrooms and green pepper rings on top. Fold dough edges over filling, pinch edges together to seal and turn placing seam side down. Allow to rise until double in size. Bake at 350 for 45 minutes. Serves 8.

Stencil or paint a wooden bowl, then polyurethane the painted area. Colorful lettuce salads will look lovely served in your new bowl!

Leisurely Lunch

Patchwork Salad

This can be made the day before.

2 16-oz. cans corn, drained
1/2 bunch broccoli flowerets
1/2 c. sweet red pepper, chopped
2 carrots, shredded
1/4 cabbage, shredded

1/4 c. salad oil
1/2 c. vinegar
1 T. sugar
salt and pepper
fresh parsley for garnish

Combine all vegetables in a large mixing bowl. In a small bowl, combine salad oil, vinegar and sugar thoroughly. Toss vegetables with dressing. Salt and pepper to taste, then garnish with fresh parsley sprigs.

Having "just the guys" for lunch? Get creative! Serve sandwiches and chips in new, clean dustpans, fabric-lined tackle boxes, or hard-hats!

Berry Fruit Toss

Serve this in a carved watermelon basket or trifle bowl.

2 qts. strawberries, sliced
2 whole pineapples, peeled,
   cored and chopped
1/2 c. orange marmalade

1/4 c. orange juice
2 T. lemon juice
1/2 c. blueberries

In a large mixing bowl, combine strawberries and pineapple; set aside. Combine orange marmalade, orange juice and lemon juice, mixing well. Add to strawberries and pineapple, combining thoroughly. Add blueberries before serving.

Hosting a bridal luncheon? Scatter confetti and small paper wedding bells on your buffet table.

Leisurely Lunch

Spinach Salad with Cilantro Dressing

Perfect for summertime! For the freshest taste, use cilantro from your own herb garden.

10 c. spinach leaves, washed
    and dried
3 oranges, peeled and sliced
1 red onion, cut into rings
1/3 c. orange juice

1/3 c. cider vinegar
1/3 c. salad oil
1/4 c. fresh cilantro, chopped
2 T. sugar

In a large bowl, combine spinach, orange slices and onion rings. Set aside. Combine remaining dressing ingredients and place in a bowl with a tight-fitting lid. Shake dressing well to combine and pour over spinach mixture; toss. Serves 6.

For a bridal shower brunch, gather lacy handkerchiefs around wax paper-covered peppermint candies or homemade chocolates, tie with a pretty bow...a lovely take-home favor!

Raspberry Cooler

Enjoy the fresh fruits of summer!

4 c. raspberries
1/2 c. sugar
1 c. water, divided

1/4 c. orange juice
1 pkg. unflavored gelatin
orange peel for garnish

Combine raspberries, sugar, 3/4 cup of water and orange juice in a blender. Mix until smooth, pour into a saucepan. Over low heat, cook for 5 minutes, then allow to cool. Combine gelatin with remaining water until thoroughly dissolved. Add gelatin to raspberry mixture, pour in a 4 cup container and freeze 2 hours. Mixture should be soft, not frozen solid. Beat mixture well and return to freezer until firm. When ready to serve, divide into desert dishes and garnish with an orange peel twist.

On the first warm day of spring, open all the windows and air out your house, turn the mattresses and put in the window screens!

Leisurely Lunch

Blackberry Fool

Easy to make and delicious! Vary the fruit with the changing summer bounty...blueberries, raspberries, or strawberries.

3 c. fresh blackberries
1/2 c. sugar
1 T. cornstarch
1 T. water
2 t. lemon juice

3-oz. pkg. cream cheese, softened
1/4 c. powdered sugar
1 t. vanilla
1/2 pt. heavy cream

Combine blackberries and sugar in a large saucepan. Heat to boiling and cook until berries are tender. Remove from heat and strain berries into a bowl. Discard any seeds. Using the same saucepan, add cornstarch and water, stirring until smooth. Fold in blackberries, stirring constantly, and continue to cook until thickened. Remove from heat and add lemon juice, stir well. Allow to cool to room temperature, place in a covered container and refrigerate until chilled. When ready to serve, spoon mixture into serving dishes. Combine cream cheese, powdered sugar and vanilla; beating until smooth. Slowly add cream, continuing to beat to a smooth texture. Place a dollop on each serving of blackberry fool, or layer in tall fluted glasses.

Summertime Lemon Cookies

A cool, lemony taste...the perfect ending for lunch!

18-oz. box lemon cake mix   2 eggs
8-oz. container whipped topping   1 c. powdered sugar

Combine cake mix, whipped topping and eggs, mixing thoroughly. Use a spoon to gather dough for each cookie, mixture will be thick and sticky. Roll spoon with dough in powered sugar and coat cookie. Use a second spoon to remove cookie. Place 2 inches apart on an ungreased cookie sheet, bake at 350 degrees until lightly golden.

Create a pretty take-home favor for guests; wrap cookies in cellophane and tuck them in a terra cotta pot with some silk sunflowers.

Leisurely Lunch

Design Your Own Garden Signs

Garden signs can be seen almost everywhere! They send cheerful messages to passersby such as "Thyme began in a Garden" or "Garden of Weedin'." It's easy to make your own sign and add your favorite saying.

Begin by buying unfinished fence posts or pickets at a lumber store, even old barn siding looks great because it's already weathered! Stain the wood or paint it a country color such as red, mustard or navy. Hand-paint or stencil your saying on, add some stars, hearts, or flowers.

Allow the paint to thoroughly dry and then spray it with a protective sealer. You can add eye hooks to the top and run wire through so your sign can hang on a fence post or wall. If you'd like to show it off in your garden, nail it to a stake and tuck in with your flowers or herbs. You can even hang one on your door that says "Gone Gardening"!

Sea Sponge Painted Pots

Create a centerpiece that coordinates with the colors of your tablecloth or dinnerware.

4 colors of acrylic paints   sea sponge
6" clay pot   paper towels
paper plates

Choose 4 acrylic paint colors that will match your dinnerware; you may even want to take a plate to the store with you. Choose a dark color for the base coat and 2 or 3 lighter colors that coordinate well. Purchase a new clay pot, or thoroughly wash an old one with steel wool and allow it to dry completely.

Give the pot 2 coats of the dark base color, allowing the paint to dry between coats. Pour a small amount of your coordinating colors on separate paper plates. Wet your sea sponge with water, then squeeze out all the excess. Dip the sponge into the paint, blotting off any excess onto a paper towel. Sponge the paint over the entire pot allowing the base coat to still show through. Let the paint dry, then sponge on a second color, again, allow the first and second paint colors to show through. Once the paint is dry you can cover the pot with a glaze for a soft luster and protection. Fill your painted pot with fresh flowers or a pillar candle.

Have lots of background music for your guests to enjoy! You can even choose music your friends will enjoy singing along to! Try oldies, classical, country, jazz, or acoustical guitar.

Leisurely Lunch

Sunny Berry Vinegar

This makes a terrific hostess gift...very unique. Gather one pint of very ripe raspberries, blueberries, blackberries, or mulberries. Wash and sterilize several clear glass jars that have very tight-fitting lids. Look at yard sales or antique shops for jars that are really pretty!

Once the jars are sterilized, add the fruit of your choice and fill the jar with vinegar. Close the jar tightly and shake well. Continue with any remaining fruit. Place your jars in a dark location for 3 weeks; remember to shake the jars daily.

After 3 weeks, strain the berries from the vinegar using cheesecloth, discard the fruit. Pour the vinegar into sterilized one-pint bottles, seal and store in a cool place. Makes 3 pints.

Some of the best things about summer: lightning bugs, crickets, flea markets, sweet corn and tomatoes, fireworks and being outdoors!

Green Apple & Eucalyptus Swag

This swag gives off a refreshing scent...perfect for welcoming spring to your home!

You'll need 12 strands of dry raffia; one yard each, a 44-inch length of thin twine, a sharp paring knife, 20 Granny Smith apples, a large bunch of flat eucalyptus and a strong needle with a large eye.

Begin by slicing each apple into 5 sections. Using the guidelines in your dehydrator, dry them until no moisture is present, but they are still pliable. An oven set at 200 degrees will also dry the apples out in 8 to 10 hours; remember to turn them frequently.

Thread your needle with the twine, tie a loop for hanging at one end. Beginning wth the eucalyptus, slide leaves onto the string and push them to the end until you have approximately 4 inches of leaves. Then slip on apple slices until you also have 4 inches. Continue to alternate leaves and apples in 4-inch sections until you reach the end of the twine. Remove the needle and tie another loop.

Use 6 strands of raffia and tie them on one end of the swag. Form a bow close to your loop; repeat with the remaining raffia.

Use your favorite cut-out cookie recipe to make ice cream sandwiches. Using the same cutter you used to make cookies, cut shapes from thick slices of hard ice cream and tuck between two cookies!

Leisurely Lunch

Spongeware Placecards

Fun for a casual gathering!

2 c. flour
1/2 c. salt
3/4 c. water
2-oz. bottles of acrylic paint in
    white, blue, red and green

foam paint brushes
sea sponges
cookie cutters
polyurethane

In a large mixing bowl, combine flour and salt. Blend in the water and stir well. As the dough becomes stiff, knead with your hands. Roll dough to a 1/4-inch thickness and cut with your favorite cookie cutters; flowers, watering cans, rabbits or stars are nice. Place "cookies" on a foil-lined baking sheet and bake at 225 degrees for 2 hours or until firm. Allow to cool completely.

Paint top and edges of the place cards with a coat of white paint; allow to dry. Dip a sponge into blue, red or green paint and gently dab the color onto the cut-outs to resemble spongeware. Set place cards aside to dry at least one hour.

When sponge painting is completely dry, write the name of each guest on a different place card with a contrasting paint color. Allow to dry one hour. To seal the paint, brush each place card with polyurethane. Place them on wax paper until thoroughly dry.

For a western lunch theme, turn a cowboy hat upside down and line with a colorful bandanna. Fill with chips, snack mix, or cornbread muffins!

Tabletop Gardens

Summer is the easiest time to create beautiful floral centerpieces. You can use cuttings from your own flower garden, or pick up blooms from a farmer's market. Delicate herbs such as dill or fennel will add fragrance as well as grace to your centerpiece.

Consider a change from the usual glass vase; watering cans, flower baskets, old-fashioned green medicine bottles, canning jars, pitchers, creamers, old glass milk bottles or galvanized tubs are wonderful!

Group your flowers and containers together to create an interesting still life. You can give a little whimsy to your arrangement by adding a straw hat, garden gloves or birdhouse.

To keep your flowers as fresh as possible, cut them early in the day or late in the afternoon. Use a sharp knife to cut the stems and then immediately place them in warm water. Remove any leaves or thorns that will be below the water level and they will last longer.

Leisurely Lunch

Windowsill Herb Garden

You can create this wonderful fragrant garden in less than one hour and have seasonings just a snip away!

To make your windowsill garden you'll need a windowbox, a plastic liner that will fit inside the windowbox, potting soil, and your favorite 4-inch potted herbs.

Punch holes in the plastic liner to allow for drainage, then place it in your windowbox. Add potting soil, continuing to fill the windowsbox until it's half full. Before planting, arrange your herbs inside the windowbox, keeping the tall-growing varieties in the back, shorter ones in the front and trailing plants toward the front and sides. When you've decided on a design you like, gently loosen the rootballs of each plant and place in the soil. Keep the plants close together to create a full look, then add more potting soil to fill the windowbox. Gently press the soil down around the plants and water well. Let any excess water drain out the bottom, and you're ready to hang your windowbox!

Your herbs will be happy in a sunny west or south-facing window and will give you a summertime full of fragrant seasonings!

This summer enjoy an old-fashioned evening ride with all the windows down. Be sure to cool off with a stop at your favorite roadside ice cream stand.

Oatmeal Sunburn Soother

Very comforting.

1 cucumber
4 c. oatmeal

2 T. rosemary leaves

In a blender, purée the cucumber well. Remove pulp from blender and place in a large mixing bowl. Add remaining ingredients and stir well; mixture will be dry and lumpy.

While running bath water, add the oatmeal blend under water faucet. Allow the mixture to blend in with the bath water, then settle in for a relaxing soak.

Take a bike ride! Gather the family together and explore nature trails, country back roads, or scenic pathways. Pack a picnic with lots of fresh juices and cool water to quench thirsts! Apples, bananas, veggies, cheese & crackers travel well. Make yummy sandwiches from thick slices of bologna on homemade bread...wonderful!

Leisurely Lunch

Citronella Potpourri

Wonderful for repelling insects at your next outdoor gathering; looks pretty too!

1 c. cedar chips
2 T. cloves
2 T. cinnamon chips
40 drops pennyroyal oil
20 drops citronella oil

20 drops eycalyptus oil
2 c. scented geranium leaves
1 c. calendula flowers
1/2 c. tansy
1/2 c. southernwood

Combine cedar chips, cloves and cinnamon chips in a large bowl; add oils. Stir well and allow scents to combine for 2 days. Add remaining ingredients mixing well. Place potpourri in several containers scattered around your patio, porch or terrace.

·You're Invited·
Garden
Tea

Garden Tea

Creamy Shrimp Spread

This looks beautiful served on bread that's been cut into circles, hearts, or triangles.

4 c. shrimp, cooked and peeled
8-oz. pkg. cream cheese, softened
1/2 c. butter
2 t. creamy horseradish

1/2 t. white pepper
1 T. lemon juice
1 t. salt
1/2 t. hot pepper sauce
1 small sweet onion, diced

Place shrimp in a food processor, blending until smooth. Remove from processor and set aside. Place remaining ingredients, except onion, in food processor, whirling until blended. Remove and combine with shrimp and onion.

All things that love the sun are out of doors.
-William Wordsworth

Watercress & Cream Cheese Sandwiches

Dainty and light...perfect for an afternoon tea!

1/3 c. fresh watercress
1/4 c. fresh parsley
8-oz. pkg. cream cheese,
  softened

1/2 stick butter, softened
2 T. chives, chopped
salt and pepper
8 slices white bread

Chop watercress and parsley in a food processor. Add cream cheese, butter, chives, salt and pepper, continue processing until mixture is thoroughly blended. Remove from food processor and spread on 4 bread slices, top with remaining slices. Using a sharp knife, cut sandwiches into quarters or triangles, or cut using a decorative cookie cutter. Place on a tray, cover and refrigerate until ready to serve.

Plant a heart-shaped garden this year using beautiful miniature roses, lemon balm, rose geranium, variegated mint, rosemary and feverfew.

Garden Tea

Apricot-Walnut Tea Sandwiches

Wonderful spread on raisin bread.

1 jar of apricot preserves
8-oz. pkg. cream cheese, softened
1/2 c. walnuts, chopped

raisin bread
mint leaves for garnish

Combine first three ingredients, blending until creamy. If desired, cut bread into circles, hearts or flowers with cookie cutters. Bread can also be cut into quarters or triangles with a sharp knife. Spread cream cheese mixture on each bread slice and garnish with mint leaves.

Strawberries and cherries are lovely when served in green Depression-era glassware.

Cucumber & Salmon Slices

Delicious salmon and dill topping.

3-oz. pkg. smoked salmon,
   flaked
1 t. lemon juice
1 t. fresh dill, chopped

1/2 c. sour cream
cucumbers
Garnish: fresh dill or parsley
   sprigs

Blend salmon, lemon juice and dill together. Place in a covered container and chill one hour. Place a design on the outside of whole cucumbers by slicing several thin strips of peel from the length of the cucumber, or scoring the peel with the tines of a fork. Cut into 1/2-inch slices. Spread with chilled salmon mixture, garnish with a fresh dill or parsley sprig. Makes approximately 48 appetizers.

Pesticide-free hollyhocks and bachelor's button blossoms add a pretty touch to your tossed salad.

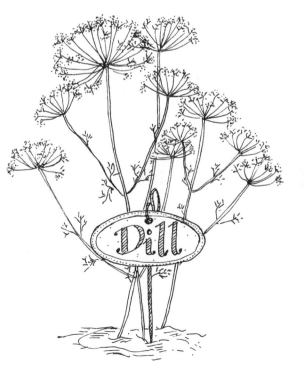

Garden Tea

English Crumpets

Simply described...a cake baked on a griddle. A forerunner of the English muffin, they're golden and delicious!

1-1/2 c. milk
1 c. water
1 pkg. active dry yeast
2 t. honey

3 c. all-purpose flour
1 t. salt
1/2 t. baking soda
1/4 c. butter, melted

Heat milk and 3/4 cup water in a saucepan over high heat. Bring to boiling, then allow to cool. Add yeast and honey to milk and let stand 5 minutes. In a separate bowl, combine flour and salt; add to milk mixture. Cover bowl and allow batter to rest until double in bulk; 1 to 2 hours. In a small bowl, combine baking soda and remaining water, beat into batter. Allow to rest 5 more minutes. Lightly oil your crumpet rings and griddle with melted butter and place rings on a medium-hot griddle. You can substitute a large cookie cutter for a crumpet ring if needed. Pour batter into rings and allow crumpets to cook until lightly golden, approximately 3 minutes. Remove rings and lightly brown crumpets on the reverse side. Repeat with remaining batter; remember to always place the batter in rings heated on the griddle first to prevent sticking. Serve warm with butter, honey or jam.

Scoop out the inside of an acorn squash and use it as a serving bowl for creamy chicken or tuna salad

Caraway & Cheddar Scones

Serve these in a pretty napkin-lined basket.

2 c. all-purpose flour
2 t. baking powder
1/4 t. salt
6 T. butter
1 c. Cheddar cheese, shredded

1 t. caraway seeds
1/3 c. bacon, fried crisp and
   crumbled
1/3 c. milk
1 egg

Lightly oil a baking sheet and set aside. Combine flour, baking powder and salt. Cut in butter until mixture is crumbly. Stir in 3/4 cup of Cheddar cheese, caraway seeds and bacon. In a small bowl, combine milk and egg, mixing thoroughly. Add to flour mixture and form a soft dough. On a lightly floured board, knead dough 5 times and roll to a 1/2-inch thickness. Using a floured biscuit cutter, cut dough and place on a lightly oiled baking sheet. Top scones with remaining cheese and bake at 425 degrees for 15 minutes or until golden. Makes approximately 18 scones.

Fill your home with spring flowers! Lots of daffodils, lilacs, and tulips bring spring inside! Put them on your table, mantle, stairsteps, sideboard and windowsill. You can even tuck a large bouquet in your empty fireplace!

Garden Tea

Apple & Celery Scones

Originally these biscuits were prepared on a hot griddle over an open fire. Although we bake them today, they're still a traditional favorite for afternoon tea.

2-1/4 c. all-purpose flour
1/2 c. sugar
2 t. baking powder
1/2 t. salt
1 stick butter
2 eggs, lightly beaten
1/4 c. milk

1 t. vanilla
1 c. apples, chopped
1/2 c. celery, chopped
1/2 t. nutmeg
1 t. cinnamon
1/4 c. brown sugar

Combine flour, sugar, baking powder and salt in a large mixing bowl. Using a pastry cutter, add butter until mixture resembles crumbs. In a separate bowl, combine eggs, milk and vanilla; stir into flour mixture. Fold in apples and celery. Drop scones by spoonfuls onto a lightly oiled baking sheet, sprinkle tops of scones with a mixture of nutmeg, cinnamon and brown sugar. Bake at 350 degrees for 30 minutes.

Serve scones or crumpets in Shaker boxes covered in floral fabric and tied with ribbon.

Lemon Tea Bread

You may want to make this a day ahead to allow the flavors to blend.

1 c. sour cream
3/4 c. sugar
1 stick butter, softened
2 eggs
1 T. poppy seeds
1 T. lemon rind, grated

2 T. lemon juice
2 c. all-purpose flour
1 t. baking powder
1 t. baking soda

In a large mixing bowl, combine sour cream, sugar and butter until fluffy. Add eggs, poppy seeds, lemon rind and lemon juice; mix thoroughly. In a separate bowl, mix together flour, baking powder and baking soda. Add to egg mixture and beat well. Pour batter into an oiled 9"x5" loaf pan and bake at 325 degrees for 45 minutes or until done. Cool before slicing.

Antique linen dresses lend a Victorian feel when hung from a clothesline.

Garden Tea

Buttery Walnut Pound Cake

A welcome addition to your garden tea party!

3 c. sugar
1 c. butter
1/2 c. solid shortening
6 large eggs
1 t. vanilla

1 c. milk
3 c. all-purpose flour
1 t. baking powder
1 c. walnuts

In a large mixing bowl, combine sugar, butter, shortening, eggs, vanilla and milk. In a separate bowl, thoroughly mix flour and baking powder; add to milk mixture. Fold in walnuts and blend. Pour batter into a lightly oiled tube pan. Bake at 325 degrees for one hour or until done.

Give a friend a notebook of watercolor paper, watercolors and brushes so she can paint her favorite flowers as they bloom.

Cranberry Tassies

Tart and crunchy...a terrific combination!

1 stick butter
3-oz. pkg. cream cheese,
   softened
1 c. all-purpose flour
1 egg

3/4 c. brown sugar
1 T. butter, melted
1 t. orange peel, grated
1/2 c. cranberries, chopped
1/2 c. pecans, chopped

In a mixing bowl, cream butter and cream cheese, stir in flour and blend well. Cover and chill for one hour. In a separate bowl, mix together egg, brown sugar, melted butter and orange peel. Fold in cranberries and pecans. Remove chilled dough from refrigerator and shape into 24 one-inch balls. Place each ball in an ungreased muffin cup; pressing dough along the bottom and up the sides. Spoon cranberry mixture into the center of each cup. Bake at 325 degrees for 30 minutes or until cranberry filling is set. Allow to cool before serving.

*Gently steep our spirits, carrying
with them dreams of flowers.
-William Wordsworth*

Garden Tea

Cinnamon Tea

Serve this tea in a crystal punch bowl with floating lemon and orange slices; add a rosemary wreath around the punch bowl base.

14 c. water
12 cinnamon herb teabags
2 c. sugar
6-oz. can frozen pineapple juice
   concentrate

6-oz. can frozen lemonade
   concentrate
6-oz. can frozen orange juice
   concentrate
6 3-inch cinnamon sticks

Bring 12 cups water to a boil, add teabags and steep for 5 minutes. Discard teabags, add remaining water, sugar, juice concentrates and cinnamon sticks. Heat through, stirring well. Serves 30.

Steep thyself in a bowl of summertime. -Virgil

Elegant Invitations

Receiving the invitation is part of the fun, so make yours memorable.
You'll need the following supplies for each invitation.

4"x3" placecard with floral
    border
black fine point calligraphy pen
8"x6-1/4" ivory cardstock
7 inches of 1-7/8" ivory organdy
    ribbon

small rubber band
small golden spoon, teacup, or
    heart shaped charm

Remove back from placecard if necessary. Using black pen, write "A Garden Tea" in the center of the placecard and glue to the center of ivory cardstock.

Fold ribbon in half and loop rubber band about an inch below the fold. To hide the rubber band, hot glue charm on top of it. When dry, glue ribbon to invitation. Slip the invitation into a matching ivory envelope closed with sealing wax and stamped with your initial.

Scatter twinkling white lights on your tabletop, across your mantle, porch, or in the trees to create a glittering, elegant mood.

Garden Tea

Come to a Garden Tea

Having a garden tea is a delightful way to enjoy the outdoors, so make yours really special. Here are some ideas to get you started.

Cover your garden furniture in lots of big fluffy pillows that encourage guests to linger in the garden. Choose patterns that compliment the colors of your garden...soft rose, sage green and lavender, or is your garden a little more bold in colors of yellow, red and purple?

Fashion a garland of peonies, roses and baby's breath to hang on your garden gate or fence. Keep them fresh by putting the flowers in tiny water vials before you weave them.

Make your table beautiful! An antique birdcage filled with flowers and topped off with flowing wired organdy ribbons makes a beautiful centerpiece!

Garnish your cake with crystallized pansies, roses, and violets...it's surprisingly easy! Gently rinse the edible blossoms and allow to dry slightly. Combine 3 tablespoons of meringue powder (found at cake decorating shops) with 6 tablespoons of warm water. Mix thoroughly until powder is dissolved. Coat each flower with meringue mixture, then dust with superfine sugar. Place on wax paper until completely dry, then arrange on your cake.

A collection of mismatched teacups make beautiful favors for your guests to take with them. Fill each teacup with water and float a single peony or rosebud inside.

Decorate the chairs at your table with garlands of fresh flowers or white netting with a length of lace wrapped around the chairback and tied in a bow.

Take pictures. A special photo serves as a sweet reminder of a wonderful outdoor gathering with friends and family.

Tie silverware together with ribbons in soft colors...peach, pink, ivory and sage are all pretty!

Fragrant Punch Bowl Wreath

Assorted herbs and flowers make this a spectacular centerpiece!

2 blocks of florist's foam   sharp knife
1 tray   fresh herbs and flowers
1 wire wreath ring

Cut foam blocks in half and firmly press into wreath ring to make
indentations on foam; remove. Using your knife, cut foam along
indentations so it will fit firmly into ring. Dip oasis sections into warm
water and allow them to soak up as much water as they can hold;
place sections into wreath ring. Place the wreath on a tray or cookie
sheet to collect any dripping water.

Cut herbs and flowers and insert into foam ring. Completely cover ring;
inside and out. Lightly mist to keep the wreath moist as you work,
refrigerate until ready to place on your table. Your wreath will stay
fresh for about one week, depending on the type of herbs and flowers.

Friendly flowers pass the hours. -Anonymous

Garden Tea

Old-Fashioned Nosegays

Victorians used these small bouquets, known as tussie mussies, to send messages to loved ones. They would be lovely in the middle of each place setting for your garden tea.

You'll need 3 plastic vials, available at a florist's shops, for each tussie mussie you'll be making. Fill each vial with water and stand them in a cup to keep them upright. Arrange your herbs and flowers in each vial. You may need to remove the plastic vial lid or use scissors to make the opening larger if needed.

Using green floral tape, wrap the 3 vials together securely, covering the full length of the vials. Cut a small hole in the center of a paper or lace doily and insert the vials through the opening. Gently bring the doily up and under the flowers. To hold the doily in place, loop a satin ribbon several times around the doily just under the flowers.

If you make your tussie mussie in advance, they will last about 2 days if you keep them in your refrigerator.

Choose flowers that have special meaning for your tussie mussie...rosemary for remembrance, lavender for devotion, or a pink rose for love.

Floral Water

An old-fashioned favorite for finger bowls. Try rose, lavender, or peppermint.

2 c. distilled water
1/4 c. vodka
1/2 c. flower petals

15 drops scented oil
square of cheesecloth

Combine water, vodka, flower petals and scented oil in a jar with a tight-fitting lid and place in a sunny location for a day to allow the heat from the sun to release the oils and color from the flowers. Using a square of cheesecloth, strain the flower petals and buds from the water. Pour into a clear bottle with a lid or cork and refrigerate. Use within 2 weeks.

Arranging a bowl of flowers in the morning can give a sense of quiet in a crowded day.
-Anne Morrow Lindbergh

Garden Tea

Rosebud Napkin Rings

So dainty and lovely! You'll need a 3-inch heart-shaped grapevine wreath, 24 to 30 small dried rosebuds and 8 inches of narrow satin ribbon.

Using a hot glue gun, carefully glue each rosebud onto the top of the heart-shaped wreath; bud tips pointing outward. Place all rosebuds then allow glue to set and cool. Fold the ribbon in half and glue to the back of the wreath at the top point. When glue has cooled, place wreath on top of folded napkin, turn napkin over and bring ribbon ends together. Tie in a bow to secure wreath to napkins.

Place violets, lily-of-the-valley and pink miniature roses in teapots to serve as centerpieces.

Rose Garden Soap

Once you have the basic recipe, you can experiment with various herb combinations....rosemary and peppermint, or lavender.

2 10-oz. bars of glycerine soap
1/2 c. rose water
1 T. anhydrous lanolin
10 drops rose oil

10 drops red food coloring
soup cans
pint-size milk cartons
vegetable oil

Over a large glass or enamel saucepan, grate soap bars. Combine with rose water and place over low heat. When the soap has melted, stir in lanolin, available at most pharmacies, and thoroughly mix; blend in rose oil. Add food coloring one drop at a time so you can control the intensity of the color. Stir well and remove from heat. Thoroughly rinse and dry soup cans and milk cartons and lightly oil the insides. Pour soap into the containers, gently tapping the sides to release any trapped air bubbles. Allow the soap to harden for 2 days before removing it from the molds. The soup cans will produce an individual-size soap, while the large bar from the milk carton can be cut into smaller, individual sizes. Allow the bars to dry until very hard.

And then my heart with pleasure fills, and dances with the daffodils.
-William Wordsworth

Garden Tea

Victorian Lavender Bag

An elegant keepsake for your guests.

6"x8" rectangle of tulle
6" of 8 inch wide double-edged
   lace

1/2 yd. of 1/2 inch wide ribbon
dried lavender

Place the tulle on the wrong side of the lace, matching the edges evenly. Fold both pieces of fabric at one time making a tube shape; keeping the tulle on the outside. Stitch the raw edges together and turn right side out.

Using half of the length of your ribbon, tie a bow around one end of the tube; fill the inside of the tube with lavender. Tie on the remaining ribbon to close the sachet.

You can dry lavender in the microwave if you're short on time. Place it on a microwave-safe plate with the microwave set at high power for 3 to 4 minutes.

Come enjoy our
Portable Menus

Portable Menus

South Street Tortilla Roll-ups

A wonderful appetizer!

8-oz. pkg. cream cheese
1 large onion, chopped
8 oz. sour cream
1 pkg. taco seasoning
8 oz. Cheddar cheese, shredded

4-1/2 oz. can green chilies
2 tomatoes, chopped
hot pepper sauce to taste
10 flour tortillas
Garnish: salsa and guacamole

Combine cream cheese, onion, sour cream and taco seasoning until smooth. Fold in cheese, chilies, tomatoes and hot sauce blending well. Spread mixture on tortillas, then roll tortillas. For easier cutting, refrigerate roll-ups until cream cheese mixture is firm. Slice and serve cold with salsa and guacamole.

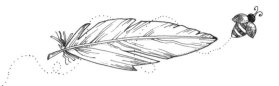

Crispy Herbed Chicken

Easy to make and ready to pack up for your picnic at a moment's notice!

1/2 c. cornmeal
1/2 c. all-purpose flour
1-1/2 t. salt
1 t. dried oregano

1/4 t. pepper
3 lb. fryer chicken, cut up
1/2 c. milk
1/3 c. butter, melted

On a large plate, combine cornmeal, flour, salt, oregano and pepper. Dip fryer pieces in milk, then thoroughly coat all sides in cornmeal mixture. Place fryer pieces in an oiled 13"x9" baking dish and drizzle butter over top. Bake for one hour at 350 degrees or until juices run clear when fryer pieces are pricked.

If you're celebrating the 4th of July with a picnic, don't forget to tuck mini flags and sparklers in your basket!

Portable Menus

Three-Bean Basil Salad

Fresh vegetables and basil from your garden will make this wonderful side dish even better!

2 c. kidney beans
2 c. garbanzo beans
2 c. green beans
1 red onion, sliced into rings
1 carrot, shredded
1/2 c. white vinegar

1/2 c. vegetable oil
6 T. sugar
1 T. fresh basil, minced
3/4 t. dry mustard
salt and pepper to taste

Drain and thoroughly rinse beans after removing from cans. Combine in a large bowl with onion and carrot. In a separate bowl, combine remaining ingredients, toss with bean mixture. Chill overnight before serving. Serves 10.

If your last picnic was at the beach, display any sea shells you collected in a clear canning jar.

Pocket Calzones

Wrap your favorite pizza toppings in these neat little pockets!

1 T. active dry yeast
1 c. warm water
1 T. honey

1/2 t. salt
3 c. all-purpose flour
favorite pizza toppings

Combine yeast, warm water, honey and salt in a bowl. Mix thoroughly until yeast is dissolved. Add 2 cups of flour, stirring until dough is smooth. Add remaining flour gradually until dough forms a ball. Knead dough on a lightly floured surface until smooth, adding more flour if dough is too sticky. Place in a lightly oiled bowl, turning once to coat dough, and allow to rise until double in bulk. Punch down dough and divide into 6 pieces. Roll each section into a 6-inch circle, fill with your favorite pizza topping; moisten dough edges and fold pastry over. Crimp edges closed with the back of a fork, pierce several holes on top. Bake at 450 degrees for 20 minutes or until golden.

For your next picnic, take along a simple bouquet arranged in an unbreakable pitcher...easy to carry!

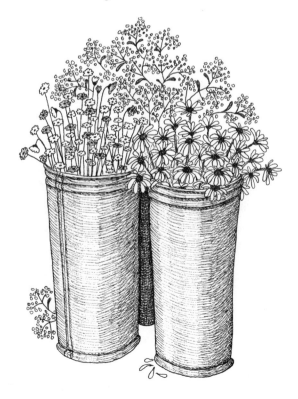

Portable Menus

Spring Salad

Pasta salad is always a hit! Pick dill early in the morning, just after the dew has evaporated.

2 c. spiral pasta
1/2 c. ripe olives, sliced
1/2 c. red onion, chopped
10 cherry tomatoes, sliced in
    half
3 carrots, sliced diagonally
1 zucchini, thinly sliced

1/2 c. green pepper, chopped
1/2 c. mayonnaise-style salad
    dressing
1/4 c. sour cream
1/2 t. garlic powder
2 t. fresh dill weed
salt and pepper to taste

Prepare spiral pasta according to directions on package. Drain, rinse and allow to cool. Combine vegetables with pasta and mix. In a small bowl, combine salad dressing, sour cream, garlic powder and dill weed mixing well. Blend into pasta and vegetables, coating thoroughly. Cover and chill one hour before serving.

For a pretty and practical hostess gift, pack a picnic basket filled with homemade salsa, pesto sauce and fresh herbs from your garden.

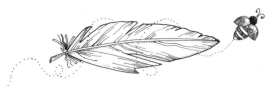

Santa Fe Pie

Just slice and eat!

10-oz. pkg. deep-dish pie crust mix
2-3/4 t. chili powder, divided
10 oz. ground chuck
1/2 c. onion, chopped
1 c. water
1-1/2 t. taco sauce
3 T. taco seasoning mix
1/3 c. ripe olives, pitted

2 oz. Monterey Jack cheese, shredded
2 oz. Cheddar cheese, shredded
2 oz. green chilies, chopped
4 medium eggs
1 c. plus 2 T. milk
1 T. flour
dash of salt
dash of cayenne

Prepare pie crust according to package directions, adding 3/4 teaspoon chili powder to mixture. Roll out dough and place in pie pan, bake as directed. Brown ground chuck and onion, draining excess fat. Add water, taco sauce, taco seasoning mix and 1-1/2 teaspoon chili powder to beef mixture; simmer 15 to 20 minutes. Blend in olives; remove from heat. Sprinkle half of the cheese in bottom of pie pan over baked pie crust. On top of cheese, layer beef, remaining cheese and chilies. In a large mixing bowl, beat eggs lightly; add milk. In a separate mixing bowl, combine flour, salt, cayenne and 1/2 teaspoon of chili powder. Add a small amount of the egg mixture to the flour mixture and whip until smooth. Add flour mixture to remaining egg-milk mix; blending well. Pour mixture over pie and bake at 375 degrees for 30 to 35 minutes.

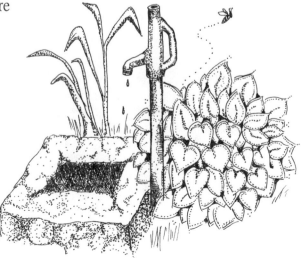

Add an old-fashioned pump and water trough to your garden to create a primitive feel.

Portable Menus

Giant Stuffed Sandwich

A meal by itself! This incredible sandwich will serve at least a dozen of your friends and family.

Dough:

1/2 c. instant oats	16-oz. box hot roll mix
1/2 c. boiling water	3/4 c. warm water
2 T. butter	2 eggs

To prepare dough, combine oats, water and butter in a mixing bowl and allow to stand for 5 minutes. Dissolve yeast from hot roll mix in warm water and combine with oat mixture, blending well. Add eggs and continue to mix well. Stir in flour mixture from hot roll mix until well blended. Form dough into a 10-inch circle and place on a lightly oiled round pizza pan. Cover with a clean cloth and allow to rise until double in bulk. Bake at 350 degrees for 30 minutes, remove from pan and allow to cool. When completely cooled, cut lengthwise.

Stuffing:

1/2 c. mayonnaise-style salad dressing	6 oz. chicken breast, cooked and thinly sliced
4 t. golden brown mustard	1 tomato, thinly sliced
8 oz. cooked honey ham, thinly sliced	1 red onion, cut into rings
6 oz. cooked peppered turkey, thinly sliced	8 slices Cheddar cheese
	shredded lettuce

Combine salad dressing and mustard, mixing well. Spread on the inside top and bottom halves of bread loaf. Layer remaining stuffing ingredients in any order desired. Replace top of loaf and cut into 12 pie-shaped wedges.

Invite your neighbors and friends over for some homemade ice cream! Have everyone bring their favorite topping to share.

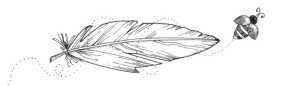

Zesty Vegetable Medley

An easy dish to prepare the night before your picnic...in the morning just pack and go!

1 c. vegetable oil
2 c. sugar
2 c. white vinegar
2 T. water
2 t. salt
1/2 t. cayenne pepper

15-oz. can peas
3 15-oz. cans green beans
1 red onion, sliced into rings
1/2 c. carrots, diced
1/2 c. zucchini, chopped

Blend oil, sugar, vinegar, water, salt and cayenne pepper and set aside. Drain and rinse canned vegetables, combine with remaining ingredients. Pour marinade mixture over vegetables, toss to coat and refrigerate overnight. Drain marinade before serving.

Instead of a large picnic basket, pack your portable picnic in small tin pails...individual lunches for everyone! Line the pails with colorful cotton dish-towels; perfect for placemats. Stick to finger foods for your menu and clean up will be a breeze.

Portable Menus

Iced Herb Tea

So refreshing in the summer heat! Try using different types of herbal tea.

6 bags peppermint herbal tea
1/2 gal. cold water

2 T. honey

Place teabags into a large pitcher, pour cold water over teabags, add honey. Place the pitcher in the refrigerator for 1 hour allowing the tea to steep. Remove teabags from pitcher before serving.

Freshly Squeezed Lemonade

Pour into a thermos and take to your next picnic.

1 c. sugar
5 c. cold water
8 lemons, juiced

Garnish: mint sprigs or lemon peel

Combine all ingredients in a large pitcher and chill. Serve in tall glasses garnished with a mint sprig or lemon peel twist.

Triple Chocolate Sour Cream Cake

A chocolate lover's dream!

1 c. all-purpose flour
1 t. baking powder
1/2 t. baking soda
1/2 t. salt
2-oz. unsweetened chocolate
   squares, broken
1 T. cocoa
1-1/4 c. sugar

1/3 c. water
2 eggs
3/4 c. butter, softened
1/2 c. sour cream
1 t. vanilla

Combine flour, baking powder, baking soda and salt in a mixing bowl. Set aside. In a food processor or blender, mix unsweetened chocolate, cocoa and sugar, process until crumbly. Bring water to a boil and add to chocolate mixture. Blend until chocolate melts. Break eggs into processor and mix well. Add butter, sour cream, vanilla and process again. Place flour mixture into food processor pulsing until all ingredients are well-blended. Lightly oil and flour an 8-inch springform pan, add cake batter. Bake at 350 degrees for one hour or until cake begins to pull away from the pan sides. When cake has cooled, remove from springform pan.

Icing:

1/2 c. heavy cream

6-oz. bittersweet chocolate
   squares, broken

Prepare icing by scalding cream in a saucepan, add bittersweet chocolate and stir for one minute. Remove pan from heat and continue to stir icing until chocolate squares are completely melted. Allow icing to cool to a warm temperature then spread on cake. Refrigerate cake to allow icing to completely set before serving.

Snackin' Cake

Perfect for packing in a picnic basket.

1 stick butter, softened	3/4 c. buttermilk
1 c. sugar	1 t. vanilla
1 egg	1 c. miniature marshmallows
2 c. all-purpose flour	1/2 c. milk chocolate chips
2 t. baking powder	1/4 c. peanut butter chips
1/2 t. salt	1/2 c. pecans, chopped

Thoroughly blend butter and sugar until creamy. Beat egg and add to butter mixture. In a separate bowl, mix flour, baking powder and salt. Set aside. In a small mixing bowl, combine buttermilk and vanilla. Alternately add dry ingredients and buttermilk mixture to the sugar mixture. Gently stir in marshmallows, chocolate chips, peanut butter chips and pecans. Pour into a greased and floured 13"x9" pan and bake at 350 degrees for 30 minutes. Cool and cut into squares. Serves 12.

Serve your Snackin' Cake in a pretty white-washed basket lined with red or blue ticking.

Picnics...Memories and Fun

The "perfect" picnic spot, the people and the food make a picnic both memorable and fun. Gather your friends and family together to celebrate a special occasion, or just escape city life and enjoy the outdoors...it's easy! We'll get you started with a basic checklist of supplies you'll need, and some picnic themes you might enjoy. The fun is up to you!

Checklist:

plates
silverware
glasses
blankets or old quilts and pillows
tablecloth
trash bags
paper towels
bottle opener
matches
flashlight & batteries
camera and film
insect repellent or citronella candles

Picnic Themes:

Breakfast Picnic...a sunny morning in a beautiful meadow
Spring Hike Picnic...tiny violets, trillium and soft sunny breezes
Family Reunion Picnic...memories, pictures, family favorites
Beach Picnic...intense blue skies, white sand and crashing waves
Garden Picnic...your own backyard, or a field of wildflowers
Moonlight Picnic...the glow of romance

If you don't have a picnic basket that's large enough, tuck all your picnic goodies in a wheelbarrow!

Portable Menus

Homespun Shaker Boxes

Pack your picnic cookies in these nostalgic boxes.

1 round wooden Shaker box
1/4 yd. homespun or ticking
   fabric

variety of buttons
1 yd. jute

Place the lid to your Shaker box on the wrong side of the homespun and using a pencil, draw the outline of the lid. Using a pair of pinking shears, cut out the circle. Spray the box lid lightly with spray adhesive and place the fabric on the lid. Quickly smooth out any wrinkles in the fabric.

Form a loose ribbon from the length of jute. Using a hot glue gun, secure the ribbon to the middle of the lid. In a random pattern, glue several sizes and shapes of buttons to the lid.

Picnics are perfect for kids! Don't forget to pack some goodies for them...books to read under your favorite tree and some crayons & paper for capturing the perfect sunny day! Disposable cameras are also a great way for kids to remember all the fun!

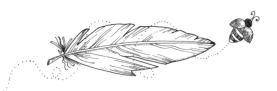

An Old-Fashioned Box Social

Turn your next picnic into a box social! In the late 19th century, box socials were popular fund raisers that combined good food with fun and a little romance.

The women would prepare and pack a lunch for two and the men would bid on the boxes. The highest bidder would share the boxed meal with the woman who had prepared it. A married man would play it safe and bid on his wife's box, while single men were probably more interested in the companionship of a young lady rather than her cooking skills.

Today you can turn any picnic into a box social. You can purchase white cake boxes at most bakeries, or gift wrap each half of a shoe box. Line the box with colorful paper napkins, and fill with an individual serving of picnic goodies. Top the boxes off with a plaid bow or small nosegay.

Pack a basket with a large quilt and plump pillows, fill a thermos with cool lemonade, add a croquet set and you're ready to take a step back in time.

Tie stacks of napkins with pretty blue and white gingham ribbon.

Portable Menus

Picnic Placemats

Make matching napkins, too!

2 yds. white fabric
wax paper
acrylic paints (red and black)
textile medium

square sponge
plate
paper towels

Machine wash fabric and press while slightly damp. Cut fabric into 16"x11" placemats. Turn the edge of each placemat under 1/2 inch, press in place. Turn raw edge under and press again; stitch in place.

Lay placemats on wax paper, smoothing out any wrinkles. In a jar, combine red paint and textile medium, following manufacturer's directions for mixing. Cut a sponge into a 2-inch square, dampen with water and squeeze out any excess. Dip sponge into red paint and textile medium mixture, blot any excess on a paper towel. Leaving a one-inch border around all edges, begin to stamp the fabric in a checkerboard pattern. Allow paint to dry.

Mix a small amount of black paint with textile medium, following manufacturer's instructions. Freehand small black ants around the remaining white border of each placemat. Allow paint to thoroughly dry, press with a hot iron to set paint.

Float whole strawberries and lime slices in your iced herbal tea, pretty!

What if it Rains?

We always envision our picnics with beautiful, sunny skies and perfect weather. However, for those times when the weather doesn't cooperate with our plans, we've come up with some alternatives you might like to try.

A picnic on the porch still lets you have the fun of eating outdoors and you'll be protected from the weather. Spread out your quilt, open the picnic basket and enjoy. You might even want to bring the guitar along!

If the weather suddenly turns chilly, a picnic in the living room can provide a cozy atmosphere. If it's a picnic for two, make it romantic with soft music and a fire in the fireplace. If it's a family affair, play some board games and toast marshmallows!

How about a 4th of July picnic...in the car! July weather can often turn hot and humid making the thought of being outdoors too much to bear. If this happens, plan a late supper picnic. Pack your picnic basket with yummy food, turn on the air conditioner and drive until you find a perfect spot for viewing fireworks. As the sun sets, enjoy your picnic in air-conditioned comfort, recline your seats and admire the fireworks display!

When you want to add a little light to your next picnic, set tea lights or votives into scallop shells.

Portable Menus

Stenciled Picnic Table

If you have an unfinished picnic table, you can turn it into a work of art in no time!

Thoroughly sand your picnic table to a smooth finish. Choose a light-colored stain and cover the picnic table, following manufacturer's directions, let dry thoroughly.

Depending upon your stencil pattern; flowers, birdhouses or ivy; choose several colors of oil paint that coordinate. Pour a small amount of stain into individual containers and lightly tint each one with a different oil paint. Place your stencils on the table top, and using a soft, clean cloth, rub the stain into the wood through the cut-outs. Carefully remove the stencil and continue. When the stain has dried completely, protect your table with a coat of water-proof varnish.

Create some clever party invitations! Paint some polka dots on plain terra cotta pots. Tuck in a plant marker that lists the time, date & place of your backyard gathering, then personally deliver your "invitations". To make a mailable invitation, glue old seed packets into handmade paper cards and tuck in some dried rose petals and lavender.

Independence Day Social

This year celebrate the 4th of July by hosting a picnic. Invite friends, neighbors and family to help you celebrate in a big way!

Make sure you can enjoy the day by preparing as many of the dishes ahead of time as possible. You can even make this picnic a potluck by providing the main dish, such as hamburgers, chicken, or a giant 6 foot sub and asking everyone else to bring their favorite side dish.

Decorate everywhere with red, white and blue! Hang old-fashioned buntings over your doorway or windows. Cover your picnic tables in red check tablecloths and serve lunch on blue spatterware dishes. White baskets filled with red carnations, blue petunias and white daisies look festive; tuck in mini flags too.

Sturdy blue spongeware crocks can hold napkins, straws, utensils or flags without blowing over, and galvanized tubs filled with ice keep sodas cool.

End the evening with an all-American old-time ice cream social! Remember all the favorites; hot fudge and butterscotch sauces, strawberries, whipped topping and nuts. Serve up your ice cream in old drugstore sundae dishes, which can still be found at flea markets and garage sales.

As the evening winds down, candlelight from punched-tin lanterns or votives tucked inside canning jars provide soft lighting while you anticipate the fireworks display to come.

Portable Menus

Crazy Softball!

While appetites are building, enjoy a spin-off of the traditional softball game! You'll need a few supplies, beginning with a collection of hats... ball caps, football helmets, straw hats, fedoras, or sombreros are fun!

On first base, place a kids' wading pool, full of water. At second base you'll need a sturdy box and a prepared, funny speech. Third base has a cardboard box or shopping bag filled with a variety of silly clothing, and home plate has a large bottle of bubbles.

The rules for your Crazy Softball game are the standard softball rules, that is if you can keep from laughing! Once a player hits the ball, he will run to first base and into the wading pool; at second, he'll stand on the box and read the funny speech. On third he'll dress-up in goofy clothing and when he makes it to home plate, blow bubbles to celebrate!

Use your imagination and have fun!

Soon the frail eggs they shall
chip, and upspringing
Make all the April woods
Merry with singing.
-Robert Louis Stevenson

ToNight

Dinner
fresh from the
Garden

Fresh from the Garden

Brown Sugar BBQ Chicken

The brown sugar makes this sauce extra special.

2-1/2 lbs. chicken pieces, cut
2 onions, sliced
1/2 c. butter
2 T. cider vinegar
1 T. Worcestershire sauce

3 t. brown sugar
1/2 t. paprika
1 c. catsup
1 c. hot water
salt and pepper to taste

Lightly oil a large baking dish and arrange chicken pieces in a single layer in pan. Place onion slices on top of chicken and dot with butter. Blend remaining ingredients together and pour over chicken. Bake covered at 350 degrees for 2 hours, uncover and bake an additional 15 minutes.

*A garden is a thing of beauty
and a job forever.
-Proverb*

Garden-Fresh New Potato Salad

Watch it disappear!

1-1/2 lbs. new potatoes, cubed
3/4 lb. fresh green beans,
  snapped
1 sweet red pepper, chopped
1 red onion, chopped
1/2 c. salad oil

1/4 c. cider vinegar
2 T. Dijon mustard
1 t. fresh parsley
1 t. fresh dill
1 t. sugar

Cook potatoes in boiling water 10 minutes, add green beans and bring to a boil. Conntinue boiling until potatoes are tender. Drain and allow to cool. In a large serving bowl, add sweet red pepper and onion to cooked potatoes and beans. Combine remaining ingredients and pour over vegetables. Toss to coat, chill thoroughly before serving. Serves 12.

You are as welcome as the flowers in May.
-Charles Macklin

Fresh from the Garden

Cheesy Philly Melt

A great grilled burger!

1 lb. ground chuck
2 T. Worcestershire sauce
4 t. dark brown mustard
1/2 t. garlic powder
1/2 t. thyme
1 medium onion, sliced into
   rings

4 oz. fresh mushrooms, sliced
2 T. butter
3-oz. pkg. cream cheese
wheat buns

Mix ground chuck with Worcestershire sauce, brown mustard, garlic powder and thyme. Combine well and shape into patties, grill until done. Sauté onions and mushrooms in butter until transparent and set aside. Spread cream cheese on wheat buns, top with onions and mushrooms.

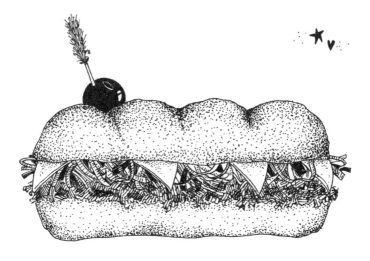

Dress your scarecrow in red, birds dislike it more than any other color.

Crunchy Cucumber Salad

This is perfect for summer potlucks!

15-oz. can chickpeas, rinsed and
    drained
1 cucumber, sliced thinly
1/2 c. ripe olives, sliced
1/2 c. sweet onion, chopped
1/4 c. fresh parsley, chopped

3 T. vegetable oil
3 T. red wine vinegar
1 T. sugar
1 T. lemon juice
salt and pepper to taste

Combine chickpeas, cucumber, olives, onion and parsley in a large
mixing bowl. Combine remaining ingredients, blending thoroughly.
Pour over salad and mix well. Serves 8.

*Create some giant bubbles! Combine 6 cups of water with 2 cups liquid deter-
gent and 3/4 cup corn syrup. Pour into a large plastic container until you're
ready to have some fun! Shape bubble wands from old coat hangers...stars,
circles or hearts are fun, then insert into a hole in the end of a dowel. Pour
bubble mixture into a shallow pan and enjoy!*

Fresh from the Garden

Country Beans & Potatoes

To keep that fresh taste, pick your vegetables right before dinner.

4 potatoes, peeled and cut into
   wedges
1 lb. fresh green beans, snapped
3 slices bacon, uncooked

1 sweet onion, cut into rings
1/4 c. fresh parsley, chopped
salt and pepper to taste

Cook potatoes in water until tender, remove from heat, drain and cool.
Place beans in a saucepan, cover with water and boil until tender.
Remove saucepan from heat, drain and rinse. Combine with potatoes.
In a large skillet, fry bacon strips for 3 minutes, add onion. Continue to
sauté until onions are transparent. Add potatoes and beans to skillet
and cook 5 minutes, sprinkle with parsley.

*If you count the number of chirps a cricket makes in 14 seconds and add 40,
it will equal the temperature!*
-Old Saying

Perfect Sweet Corn

Everyone has their own opinion...this is how we like it best!

When you buy corn, look for fresh corn with bright green husks and plump kernels. If the kernels are dry looking and the husks are a deep green, the corn probably isn't fresh. Remember to refrigerate corn as soon as you get it home.

When you're ready to serve your corn, place a large stockpot on the stove, fill it with water and bring to a boil. Husk the corn and add ears to the boiling water...you may want to use tongs to keep from being splashed with hot water. Cover the stockpot and as soon as the water begins to boil again, remove it from the heat. Allow the corn to sit 5 minutes, uncover and enjoy! You can keep the corn warm in the hot water for up to 10 minutes without it becoming tough. Dot it with fresh herb butter and enjoy!

Herb Butter

1 c. butter, softened   1 t. dried rosemary
1 t. dried marjoram   1/4 t. garlic powder

Using a hand-held mixer, beat all ingredients together until thoroughly blended. Place in a container with a tight-fitting cover and refrigerate until ready to use.

Fresh from the Garden

Harvest Casserole

Full of wonderful vegetables from your own backyard!

1 T. fresh sage, chopped
4 red potatoes, cut in 1/4-inch
   thick wedges
1/4 c. butter
3 sweet red peppers, chopped

1 yellow onion, sliced
2 large zucchini, thinly sliced
1/2 c. long-grain rice, cooked
4-oz. pkg. Cheddar cheese,
   shredded

Wash sage thoroughly, chop and set aside. Place potatoes in a lightly-oiled 2-1/2 quart casserole. Dot the potatoes with half the butter, then sprinkle on half the sage, peppers, onion, zucchini and rice. Layer ingredients again, cover with foil and bake at 350 degrees for one to 2 hours, or until potatoes are tender. Remove foil, sprinkle cheese over top, and return to oven until cheese is melted. Cool slightly before serving. Serves 6.

Transform an unwelcome tree stump into an herb garden! Mound dirt over the stump and surround it with large rocks. Plant thyme, oregano, chives, sage, or any of your other favorites.

Crazy Quilt Strawberry-Rhubarb Pie

The crust is half the fun!

1 double crust, deep dish pie
  crust, your favorite recipe
3 c. fresh rhubarb, sliced
3 c. fresh strawberries, sliced

1 c. sugar
1-1/2 T. instant tapioca
1/3 c. orange juice

Prepare your favorite deep dish, double crust pie crust recipe. Place bottom pie crust in pie pan and set aside. Using a pastry wheel, cut top crust into lattice strips. Set aside. Combine remaining ingredients in a large mixing bowl and let stand 20 minutes. Pour into bottom pie crust. Place lattice strips in random "crazy quilt" style on top of the pie filling. Bake for 20 minutes at 400 degrees, reduce heat to 375 degrees and bake an additional 30 minutes.

*Oh happy garden! Whose seclusion deep hath been so friendly
to industrious hours.*
-William Wordsworth

Fresh from the Garden

Apple Cake with Cinnamon Sauce

Try this with Gala or Jonathan apples for a change in taste.

1-1/2 c. oil
2 c. sugar
4 eggs
2-1/2 c. all-purpose flour
2 t. baking powder

1 t. cinnamon
3 c. Red Delicious apples, peeled
   and chopped
1 t. vanilla

Mix together oil and sugar. Beat in eggs one at a time. In a separate bowl, combine flour, baking powder and cinnamon, blend into egg mixture. Fold in apples and vanilla, mix thoroughly. Oil and flour a tube pan and bake for one hour at 350 degrees. Cool, remove from pan and serve with Cinnamon Sauce.

Cinnamon Sauce:

4 T. butter
2 c. brown sugar
1-1/2 t. cinnamon
2 c. water, boiling

4 T. all-purpose flour
1 t. salt
2 t. vanilla

Combine all ingredients in a saucepan and bring to a boil, stirring constantly. Serve warm over slices of Apple Cake.

The ornament of a house is the friends who frequent it.
-Ralph Waldo Emerson

Country Apple Cooler

Serve with a sprig of mint.

8 bags cinnamon herbal tea
1 qt. boiling water
12-oz. can frozen apple juice
    concentrate

1 apple, sliced
3 6-inch cinnamon sticks

Add teabags to boiling water, allow to steep 5 minutes. Remove teabags from water, add apple juice concentrate. Fill apple juice can 3 times with cold water and pour into tea mixture. Serve in tall glasses over ice. Add apple slices and cinnamon sticks as a garnish.

Worn out work boots, garden shoes and even tennis shoes can be filled with dirt and serve as clever flowerpots!

Fresh from the Garden

Colorful Country Napkins

When there's all this wonderful country cooking, there's bound to be some spills. Why use paper napkins when you can have colorful, easy-care cotton bandannas!

They're inexpensive, come in a variety of colors and their large lap-covering size makes them perfect! Slip a wooden clothespin around each one to keep them from blowing away, or tuck them into tall glasses or baskets.

For a special dinner, line your porch steps with sweet-smelling citronella candles. In the fall...get out your plaid stadium blanket and enjoy a midnight dinner on the porch amongst the glow of sparkling carved pumpkins.

Decorative Pie Crusts

In addition to our Crazy Quilt pie crust on page 95, here are two easy ways to add a decorative touch to your homemade pies.

Appliqué Pies:

Roll out the dough as you normally would for a top crust; lay it over the pie filling, trim and crimp the edges. Gather any remaining scraps and reroll the dough to a 3/8-inch thickness for the appliqué designs. Using a sharp knife, cut out shapes such as leaves, pears or apples. Brush the bottom of the cut-outs lightly with water and place on the pie top before baking. Really pretty!

Stained Glass Pies:

Gather your favorite small cookie cutters...stars, hearts, flowers or leaves are pretty. Roll your top crust as usual and make cutouts in the dough before placing it over the pie filling. They'll not only be pretty, they'll serve as steam vents too!

Try making a starburst edge on your next pie crust! Just trim the dough even with the edge of the pie pan and cut the crust at 1/2-inch intervals, 1/2 inch long. Fold each square diagonally to the side to create a triangle. A really pretty finishing touch for your favorite pie!

Fresh from the Garden

Trompe L'oeil

Turn an old garden shed or milk house into a whimsical garden accent; create an illusion with trompe l'oeil. This style of painting became popular in Greece and Rome when it was used to create the illusion of formal architecture where none existed.

Today you can rag or sponge color onto a surface to look like brick, stucco or stone. Tuck in fun designs such as watering cans, flowers, seed packets, birds, garden tools, or birdhouses. You can paint on larger elements such as shutters or windowboxes also. If you'd like more detail in your design, stencil or free-hand vines and flowers or seed packets. Always use weather-resistant, colorfast primers and latex paint. Let your imagination go!

Give an old garden bench more character by adding a birdhouse or grapevine wreath to its seat.

Quick Kitchen Seasonings

Create these easy-to-make seasoning mixes from your herb garden now and they'll make wonderful hostess gifts this holiday season!

Popcorn Mix:

Combine equal portions of dried basil, dried oregano, dried parsley, onion powder and garlic salt, mixing well. Add one tablespoon of this mixture to 1/2 cup of melted butter, pour over popcorn.

Spicy Pepper Mix:

In a bowl, combine equal parts of green peppercorns, white peppercorns, black peppercorns, dried red bell peppers, parsley and sea salt. Run through a pepper grinder and store in a dry location until ready to use.

No-Salt Herb Blend:

4 T. dried basil	4 T. dried savory
4 T. dried oregano	4 t. garlic powder
4 t. onion powder	2 t. dried thyme
2 t. dried rosemary	1 t. dried sage
1 t. black pepper	

Crumble all dried herbs, removing any stems. Place herb mix in a container with a tight-fitting lid until ready to use. Great for sprinkling in pasta sauces or on grilled dishes.

Those who can, garden; and those who garden, can.

-Anonymous

Fresh from the Garden

Vegetable Centerpieces

Use the beauty found in your garden to dress up your table…easy and fast! Collect a variety of clay pots in all sizes. Group them on your sideboard or in the center of your serving table. Place tall clay pots in the back and the smaller ones in the front and on the sides. Wash and dry a variety of vegetables from your garden, then fill each pot with a different color and size of vegetable.

Cauliflower and broccoli look great in large pots, while green beans, carrots and scallions can stand upright in smaller pots. Cherry tomatoes, Brussel sprouts and radishes form a tall centerpiece when piled high. This quick arrangement can stay on display for a day or two and still look fresh.

An old rainbarrel can be a clever storage spot for rakes, shovels, hoes or any large gardening tool.

Share Nature's Bounty

We gain so much more than just fresh produce when we plant a garden. There's a pleasure that comes from tilling the earth, in addition to some good exercise, that we can all enjoy. We all know someone who could share in our harvest, so why not add one more row in your vegetable garden? Most of us can squeeze in an extra row even if our space is limited.

When harvest time comes, share that extra row of green beans or tomatoes with an elderly neighbor who is housebound, or someone without the means to buy fresh vegetables. It will be appreciated more than you'll ever know. This year, make your motto: "Share Nature's Bounty."

Fill a coffee can with warm water. Melt a pound of butter and add to the coffee can. Submerge an ear of corn into the can and when you pull the ear back out the butter will stay on the corn!

Fresh from the Garden

Making a Scarecrow

A simple, old-fashioned project that only requires imagination and time.

Although he may not protect your vegetable patch, making a scarecrow is a wonderful project for all ages! Rummage through your closet to find old clothing: jeans, plaid shirt and a straw hat for a gentleman; a dress, jewelry, hat and gloves for Mrs. Scarecrow.

Begin by stuffing an old pair of panty hose with rags; stitch the opening closed. Repeat with a second pair of panty hose; then sew the two waists together to form the body.

Put a pair of old pants or jeans over one pair of legs. The shirt will go over the arms; button it up and tie string around the shirt cuffs. Next, give your scarecrow a face by painting a pumpkin with fast-drying acrylic paint.

Create a T-shape from 2 lengths of wood, leaving a long enough portion at the top to attach your pumpkin head. Place the pole down the back of your scarecrow's shirt, drape his arms over the T-shape. Tap the pole into the ground until it's firmly set. Make a hole in the bottom of the pumpkin and place it on top of the T-shape. Give him a straw hat, a pair of gloves and tuck some straw in shirt or pantleg openings for decoration.

Shoo-hoo, shoo-hoo!
away, birds, away. Take a corn
and leave a corn and come no
more today!
-Old Scarecrow Song

Wheelbarrow Gardens

As silly as it may sound, gardening in a wheelbarrow is the perfect way to get a jump on spring! Not only is your garden portable, but by planting in your wheelbarrow the soil warms up faster in the spring, and doesn't freeze as early in the fall.

Good drainage is important for your garden. You'll need to spread the bottom of the wheelbarrow with 2 inches of pebbles, or drill several holes in the bottom. Add 8 inches of potting soil and lightly mist with water. Sprinkle your seeds; lettuce, spinach, parsley and cilantro are good choices, and lightly cover with soil.

Your seeds will germinate quickly if you cover your wheelbarrow with clear plastic and keep the soil moist. Keep your wheelbarrow in a sunny location, but remember to protect it from heavy rains that will flood your plants. Soon you'll be able to harvest your plants all summer long!

If, while working in the garden your rake falls prongs upward, there will be a
heavy rain the next day.
-Old Saying

Fresh from the Garden

Vintage Silverware Wind Chimes

*Odd pieces of silver or silver-plated flatware can be found
inexpensively at flea markets or thrift stores.*

2 dinner forks   1 dessert fork
1 butter knife   fishing line, 30 lb. weight
2 spoons

Using a drill with a 1/16-inch drill bit, drill a hole in the handle of each
silverware piece, approximately 1/4 inch from the ends of the handle.
Smooth any rough edges with an emery cloth if needed. Drill a hole in
one dinner fork 1/4 inch above the fork tines. This will serve as the
main support for the wind chime.

Using a pair of needlenose pliers, bend the tines on both dinner forks
in a north, south, east and west direction, forming a small
loop on the edge of each tine. Insert a length of fishing
line through the hole in the main support fork handle,
this will allow you to hang your chime. On the same
fork, attach 5 inches of line in the hole above the
tines, and slip through the hole in the handle on the
second dinner fork which will serve as the center
chime. Using approximately 7 inches of line, tie and
suspend each of the remaining pieces of silverware
to a separate tine loop on the top support. Adjust
the line if needed so the silverware strikes against
the center chime.

*Display flowers in new ways…a child's wagon, a
flat-backed basket on your door, an old wooden
toolbox, crystal decanters or antique silver
cruet sets all make unique displays!*

Straight-From-the-Garden Wreath

This wreath is a colorful combination of your garden produce and it's so simple to make! Harvest asparagus, green onions, carrots, green beans, radishes and beets from your garden; wash them well and pat dry.

Begin your wreath by separating the vegetables into groups. Gather a handful of green beans and bunch them together with a long strand of raffia. Wrap the raffia several times around your beans and tie off with a knot. Repeat with groups of the remaining vegetables. You'll find that for larger vegetables, such as beets and carrots, you'll only need 2 or 3 tied together.

Using florist's wire, wire each group of vegetables onto a straw wreath base. Turn the vegetables at different angles and overlap them to make your wreath interesting. Tuck in a few fresh herbs such as variegated sage or mint and you'll have a beautiful wreath for your kitchen door!

Fresh from the Garden

Floral Skin Refresher

Refreshes your skin.

1 c. apple cider vinegar
2 T. rosemary
4 T. sage leaves

5 T. rose petals
3/4 c. rosewater

Because vinegar reacts with metal, place herbs in a quart-size glass jar with a cork or other non-metallic lid. In a glass saucepan, bring vinegar just to simmering and pour into jar of herbs. Tighten down lid and combine mixture by shaking the jar daily for 10 days. At the end of 10 days, strain the herbs and add rosewater. Store in decorative jars with tight-fitting corks or non-metallic lids.

A heart-shaped box filled with dried roses is a charming gift for a friend.

- PLEASE JOIN US FOR -

Mouth-Watering
Grilled
Dishes

Grilled Dishes

Shrimp Kabobs

Ready to eat in minutes!

3 carrots, cut diagonally
1 green pepper, cut into 1" strips
1/4 c. water
1/2 t. orange peel, grated

1/2 c. orange juice
2 t. canola oil
2 t. fresh thyme, minced
12 shrimp, peeled and deveined

Combine carrots, green pepper and water in a saucepan. Bring to a boil, cover and simmer 3 minutes. In a small bowl, combine orange peel, orange juice, oil and thyme. Set aside. Lightly oil your grill or broiler pan with non-stick spray. Skewer shrimp, carrots and peppers and place on grill. Baste kabobs with orange juice mixture and grill 2 minutes; 3 inches from the heat. Turn kabobs, baste again and grill another 3 minutes or until shrimp turn pink.

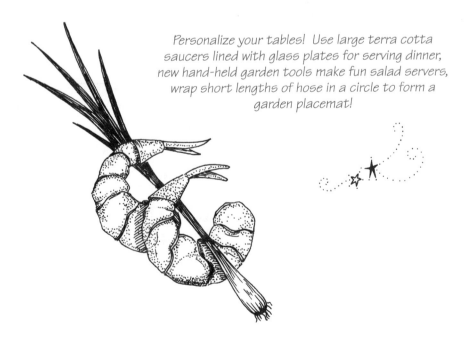

Personalize your tables! Use large terra cotta saucers lined with glass plates for serving dinner, new hand-held garden tools make fun salad servers, wrap short lengths of hose in a circle to form a garden placemat!

Hot & Spicy Ginger Chicken

Serve your remaining marinade as a sauce for dipping.

1/2 c. water
5 slices fresh ginger
2 dried chili peppers, crumbled
1/2 c. onion, chopped
1/4 c. white vinegar
1 T. hot pepper sauce

1 t. dried thyme
1/2 t. ground allspice
1/2 t. ground black pepper
1-1/2 lbs. boneless, skinless
    chicken breasts, cubed

Purée water, ginger, chili peppers, onions, vinegar, pepper sauce thyme, allspice and black pepper in a blender. Pour marinade into a large mixing bowl, add chicken, tossing gently to cover and refrigerate for 4 hours. Remove chicken from mixing bowl, reserving marinade. Bring marinade to a boil in a small saucepan, then transfer to a serving bowl to be used for dipping. Skewer chicken and grill 5 minutes on each side. Wonderful served on a bed of rice with fresh fruit.

For a quick, cool dessert, layer blackberries, vanilla yogurt and crushed graham crackers in a crystal bowl.

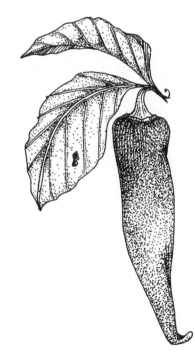

Grilled Dishes

Red Snapper with Fennel

Harvest your fennel branches a few days before grilling to allow it time to dry out.

dried fennel branches
1 stick butter

juice of 1 lime
1-1/2 lbs. red snapper, cleaned

Prepare grill by placing coals in grill and topping with fennel branches. Bring grill to medium heat while preparing the marinade. Melt butter in a saucepan, remove from heat and add lime juice, mixing well. Place red snapper on a lightly oiled grill, baste with lime marinade and grill 10 minutes. Turn red snapper, baste and grill 10 minutes more or until completely cooked through. Remaining marinade can be used as a dipping sauce.

Is someone in your family going on a trip or off to college? Keep the party theme by using old suitcases and trunks that are no longer useful. Line them with plastic and fill with ice and soda cans! You can also use smaller suitcases to stack plastic flatware and napkins in!

Lemon Rice

Perfect with grilled snapper.

2 t. olive oil
1 c. onion, finely chopped
1 c. mushrooms, sliced
1-3/4 c. long-grain rice,
    uncooked

3 c. hot water
1 T. lemon rind, grated
2 t. fresh oregano, chopped
2 T. lemon juice

Add oil to a large skillet over medium heat. Sauté onion and mushrooms until tender. Add rice and sauté one minute. Pour in hot water, lemon rind and oregano. Place lid on skillet and simmer for 10 minutes or until liquid has evaporated. Remove from heat. Add lemon juice and fluff before serving.

Line a colander with sheet moss and fill with dirt; add trailing petunias and vinca vines; attach a plant hanger and you have a clever hanging basket!

Roasted Sweet Peppers

For a different taste, try red or yellow peppers.

2 green peppers
2 T. olive oil
1 c. green onions, diced
4-oz. pkg. fresh mushrooms,
   sliced

1-1/2 t. fresh thyme
1/4 c. couscous
2 T. water
2 plum tomatoes, chopped

Remove top third from peppers, seed and rinse well. Lightly oil a baking dish and set aside. Place one tablespoon of oil in an oven-proof skillet and heat to medium-high. Add green onions and mushrooms, sauté 5 minutes. To skillet mixture add thyme, couscous and water, blending well. Remove skillet from heat and stir in tomatoes. Stuff peppers with couscous mixture and arrange peppers in an oiled baking dish. Place in a preheated oven at 400 degrees and roast stuffed peppers 35 minutes or until tender. Serves 2.

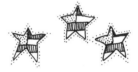

Hosting a barbecue for a graduating senior? Provide plain T-shirts and fabric pens for grads to write notes to each other on! Encourage them to keep in touch by providing an address book.

Garden Patch Grilled Vegetables

Gather your garden's bounty and begin!

6 small onions
1 lb. carrots, cut diagonally
4 potatoes, cut into wedges
1 sweet red pepper
1 green pepper

1/2 c. olive oil
fresh thyme
1 zucchini, cut into rounds
4 oz. mushrooms
salt and pepper to taste

Place onions, carrots and potatoes in a saucepan, cover with water and cook until crisp-tender; after approximately 15 to 20 minutes, remove from heat and drain. Cut peppers, seed and slice into strips. In a mixing bowl combine oil and thyme. Combine all vegetables in a large bowl and coat with oil mixture. Remove vegetables from oil and place on grill at medium heat. Use remaining oil mixture to brush on vegetables as they grill to prevent sticking. Turn the vegetables often, removing when tender and browned. Sprinkle with salt and pepper if desired.

Grilled Dishes

Sea Scallops

So tender when grilled!

2 T. lime juice
1 T. canola oil
1 garlic clove, crushed
1/2 t. ground cumin

1/8 t. cayenne pepper
1 lb. sea scallops
2 c. cherry tomatoes

Prepare marinade by combining lime juice, oil, garlic, cumin and cayenne pepper together in a medium mixing bowl. Whisk thoroughly. Alternately place scallops and tomatoes on metal skewers and brush on marinade. Place skewers on a platter, cover and refrigerate 30 minutes. Grill scallops 5 to 7 minutes, basting with marinade. Serves 4.

Set your table with a nautical theme! Decorate with a blue tablecloth, cheery red napkins and placemats, cobalt blue tumblers and white dishes! Create a centerpiece from an old bucket filled with sand and shells, tuck a candle in the middle. Intertwine white roping across the top of the table and tuck tea lights into small shells.

Rosemary Corn

For the freshest taste, pick corn from your garden then rush it to the grill!

12 ears of sweet corn
1 stick butter, melted

2 t. fresh rosemary, chopped

On each ear of corn, pull the husk back without completely removing it. Remove silk and rinse corn and husks thoroughly under cool running water. Combine butter and rosemary, blending well. Using a basting brush, coat each ear of corn with butter mixture; pull the husks back over the ear of corn. Place corn on grill over medium heat and grill approximately 20 minutes. Turn ears frequently for even grilling.

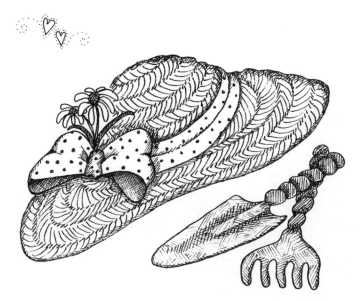

Take time for an afternoon nap in a hammock!

Grilled Dishes

Sunflower Slaw

Crisp, sweet and crunchy!

5 carrots, shredded to equal 3
   cups
4 oz. sunflower seeds, lightly
   toasted
1-1/2 c. pineapple chunks,
   drained

1 head of cabbage, shredded
2-1/2 T. lemon juice
2-1/2 T. orange juice
3/4 c. mayonnaise

In a large bowl combine carrots, sunflower seeds, pineapple chunks
and cabbage, toss well. In a separate bowl combine remaining ingredients, blending well. Pour over cabbage mixture and toss to coat.
Serves 6.

Have fun decorating the buffet
table for your sports-minded
guests! Fill a thermos with
water and fresh daisies, place
it in a wire basket and
surround it with tennis balls.
Place napkins and flatware in
empty tennis ball cans tied
with new shoestrings!

Grilled Herb Bread

Try different herb combinations...marjoram, chives or basil.

2 c. warm water
2 pkgs. yeast
1/3 c. plus 1 t. sugar
1/3 c. oil

2 t. salt
6 c. all-purpose flour
1/4 c. chopped herbs

Combine water, yeast and one teaspoon of sugar in a mixing bowl; allow to sit 10 minutes. Gently stir in remaining sugar, oil and salt. Add 3 cups flour and stir. Gradually add remaining flour one cup at a time, working well. Place dough on a lightly floured surface and knead, adding more flour if sticky. Lightly oil a large bowl and place dough inside. Turn dough once to coat with oil. Allow to rise until double in bulk. Before rolling dough out, oil rolling pin and work surface. Cut dough in half and roll out to a 1/4-inch thickness. Repeat with remaining half. Coat one side of dough with oil and place on grill, oiled side down. Oil top side and sprinkle on herbs to taste. Allow bread to grill 2 minutes, flip and grill another 2 minutes or until golden.

Pick a spot next to your patio or picnic area and place two trellises, the type with square openings, in the ground one in front of the other. If they're about 6 inches apart they'll create an outdoor "wine rack" for your sparkling water or fruit juices; perfect for your next outdoor get-together!

Grilled Dishes

Zesty Onion Relish

A wonderful condiment for chicken, pork, or beef.

2 lbs. large onions, sliced thick
1/4 c. canola oil
3 T. balsamic vinegar

2 T. brown sugar
1/4 t. cayenne pepper

Lightly brush onion slices on each side with oil. Place onions on grill and cook over low heat for 15 minutes or until tender and golden. Turn onions to brown each side, coating again with oil as needed. Remove onions from grill and allow to cool. Chop onions and set aside. Simmer vinegar and brown sugar in a saucepan over low heat. Stir until sugar has dissolved then pour over onions. Sprinkle cayenne pepper over top and stir again. Serve warm, refrigerating any leftovers.

Serve your Zesty Onion Relish in a small glazed terra cotta pot tied with a cheery gingham ribbon.

Raspberry Sun Tea

Let the sun do all the work!

6 raspberry herb teabags
3 qts. cold water

1/4 c. sugar
fresh mint sprigs for garnish

Put teabags into a one gallon glass container, add cold water. Set the container on your sunny porch, patio or windowsill for several hours. Remove teabags, add sugar to taste, stir well and chill. Pour into tall, chilled glasses filled with ice; garnish with mint sprigs.

Float pretty raspberry ice cubes in your sun tea! Fill each compartment in an ice-cube tray half full of water; freeze. Remove from the freezer and put a fresh, whole raspberry on each ice cube, anchoring it with a teaspoon of water; refreeze. Fill compartments with water and freeze until solid. Lovely floating in your pitcher!

Key Lime Pie

Cool and tangy...perfect after a grilled dinner.

4 extra-large eggs, separated
14-oz. can sweetened condensed
   milk
1/4 c. key lime juice

8-inch pie shell, baked
1/4 t. cream of tartar
1/4 c. sugar

Using an electric beater, beat egg yolks until foamy, add condensed milk, blending thoroughly. Add lime juice and continue to beat until mixture is thick. Pour into baked pie shell and bake at 350 degrees until filling is set, approximately 10 minutes. Remove from oven and allow to cool completely. In a small bowl, beat egg whites until foamy, blend in cream of tartar. Slowly add sugar and continue to beat until egg whites are stiff; then spread on pie. Bake at 450 degrees until meringue is golden.

After a sizzling barbecue meal, cool off with an assortment of frosty treats!
Keep them cool by filling a small wagon with crushed ice and lots of fruit pops
and ice cream sandwiches! Wrap them in clear plastic
and tie with colorful ribbons!

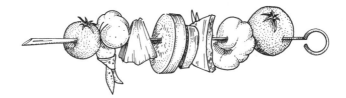

Flowerpot Placecards

These make wonderful accents for your outdoor table! Fill a simple clay pot with soil and sprinkle grass seed over the top; rye grass is a really fast growing variety. After planting the seeds, put your clay pots in a bright window and water when the soil feels dry to the touch.

Within 2 weeks the grass will be tall enough for you to move outdoors to your table or patio. When the grass begins to get too tall, simply clip it back with a pair of scissors. Using a permanent marker, write your guests' names on garden markers and place in each flowerpot.

If you want to add some flowers from your garden, simply pick your favorite blossoms and tuck the stems into plastic water vials, available at florists' shops. Arrange the vials in your grass pot deep enough to hide the vial; then gently press the vials into the soil. A unique summer accent!

Perk up your outdoor furniture with some new cushions!

Grilled Dishes

"Stained Glass" Luminarias

These give a festive look to your deck or patio! Keep the colors fun and bright...yellow, pink, purple and blue look terrific together.

glass containers, any size
tissue paper
decoupage medium

foam brush
aerosol acrylic sealer

Choose a variety of glass containers; rose or fish bowls are just the right size. Cut your tissue paper into several geometric shapes, varying the sizes. Using a foam brush, apply a thin layer of decoupage medium to a piece of tissue paper. Place the tissue paper on the outside of your glass container and gently smooth out any wrinkles. Continue with remaining pieces of tissue paper alternating shapes and colors and overlapping them until the container is completely covered. Be sure and wrap the paper over the top of the rim also.

When tissue paper has dried, apply a light coat of acrylic sealer and let dry. Apply a second coat, dry thoroughly. Place a candle in a votive holder and set inside the luminaria. When the candles are lit, the candlelight will softly glow through the paper.

Invite a new neighbor to your outdoor gathering! Fill a pretty box with quick breads, preserves, pancake mix and syrup. Tuck in maps and brochures suggesting new things to do around their new home. They'll meet new friends and feel so welcome!

Marinades & Rubs

These can bring out the best in a cut of meat, poultry, or fish. Here's a variety of easy-to-make marinades for your next backyard gathering.

Jamaican Spice Rub

1/4 c. cumin seeds
2 T. coriander seeds
2 T. chili powder
1 T. light brown sugar

2 T. kosher salt
1 t. cinnamon
1 t. cayenne pepper
2 T. black pepper

Toast seeds in an ungreased skillet over low heat for 2 minutes. Place in a grinder and add remaining ingredients. Process until mixture becomes a powder. Can be stored at room temperature for 2 months.

Balsamic Marinade

1/2 c. balsamic vinegar
2 T. scallions, chopped
1 T. sage, chopped

1 T. rosemary, chopped
1 c. olive oil

Combine vinegar, scallions, sage and rosemary in a food processor. Pulse and add oil until fully blended and smooth.

Score the skin of chicken and fish before marinating so they can better absorb the flavor of the spices.

Grilled Dishes

Firing up the Grill

A grill temperature that's perfect for chicken can ruin fish. Here's some suggestions to keep in mind before you grill.

Moderate heat works best for grilling vegetables, poultry, pork, Italian sausage or bratwurst and thick fish filets. A moderately warm grill will help cook these foods thoroughly without burning them.

High heat will sear the outside and form a nice crust without over-cooking the center. High heat is best for steak, shellfish and thin fish filets.

Remember that all meat, fish and poultry will cook evenly if they're brought to room temperature before grilling.

A good guideline for how much marinade to use is one cup for every 2 to 3 pounds of meat, poultry or fish; if it's very strong or sweet, simply brush it on the food you're grilling. Allow one tablespoon of spice rub for each serving.

Salsa Garden

Have fun with this garden plan! Not only is it easy to create, you'll find there's nothing like the taste of fresh salsa!

Choose the size of your garden, and we'll give you a list of the plants to get you started; plus an easy recipe.

tomatoes
jalapeño peppers
Habañero chile peppers
cilantro
Spanish yellow onions
Hungarian wax peppers
tomatilloes

Spicy Red Salsa:

1 large tomato, chopped
1 small onion, chopped
1 tomatillo, chopped
1 jalapeño pepper, chopped

1 T. fresh cilantro
1 t. lime juice
1/4 t. salt

Combine all ingredients in a small mixing bowl, stirring gently to mix. Refrigerate in a covered container for one hour. Leftovers will remain fresh for one week if refrigerated. Makes 2 cups.

Grilled Dishes

Savory Smoke

Although mesquite is the most popular wood for the grill, different types of wood impart different flavors to the food you're grilling. Oak is best for ham, beef and game, while hickory is best for pork, chicken and turkey.

Wood from fruit trees, such as apple or cherry, gives a sweet flavor to mild foods such as chicken and shellfish. Mesquite has a sharp flavor and is best with beef, pork and thick fish fillets.

Grapevine cuttings will give off a mild aroma that's nice for poultry and fish. Before grilling, soak the grapevines in water and then place them in the hot fire for the last 10 minutes of grilling.

Dried corncobs whose kernels have been removed, will give grilled foods a hickory flavor. Pecans, walnuts, or almonds will also add a distinct flavor to grilled foods. Before using nuts, soak them briefly and partially crack their shells.

Herbs from your garden add a great taste to grilled dishes. Soak rosemary, dill, or tarragon in water for half an hour then toss them on the hot coals.

Make a grapevine "windsock" for your porch! Tie 18-inch lengths of craft ribbon in assorted colors to a grapevine wreath; attach a wire plant hanger and hang from a ceiling hook. So festive as the streamers blow in the breeze!

Summer Watermelon Centerpiece

Colorful flowers and cool watermelon make an unusual but terrific summer centerpiece!

1 small to medium watermelon   florist's foam block
Rosea evening primrose flowers   green florist's tape
sweet pea flowers

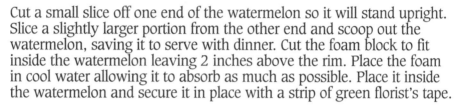

Cut a small slice off one end of the watermelon so it will stand upright. Slice a slightly larger portion from the other end and scoop out the watermelon, saving it to serve with dinner. Cut the foam block to fit inside the watermelon leaving 2 inches above the rim. Place the foam in cool water allowing it to absorb as much as possible. Place it inside the watermelon and secure it in place with a strip of green florist's tape.

Arrange the longest stems of the primrose in the back of the foam. Cut some shorter and place them around the middle. Fill in around the edges with sweet peas, allowing some to trail over the edges. Add variety to your arrangement by alternating sweet pea colors of pink, salmon, lavender and ivory.

Attach a strand of cool-burning light bulbs to the underside of a patio table umbrella to create a lantern effect.

Grilled Dishes

Quick & Easy Summer Jams

Your friends and family will think you spent hours making these flavorful jams...only you'll know they're a snap to make!

Blackberry Jam:

1-3/4 c. fresh blackberries   1/4 c. sugar

Mix berries and sugar together in a 6-cup microwave-safe bowl. Microwave on high for 6 minutes; let cool. Place in a pretty jelly jar, cover and refrigerate. Will keep several weeks refrigerated.

Peach Jam:

2 medium peaches   1/4 c. sugar

Pit and purée peaches in a food processor. Mix with sugar. Microwave 6 minutes on high power; allow to cool. Transfer jam to to a covered container and refrigerate. Jam will stay fresh several weeks. Makes 1-1/4 cups.

Lemon-Lime Marmalade

1 medium lemon   3/4 c. sugar
1 medium lime

Quarter, seed and purée lemon and lime. Mix with sugar and transfer to a microwave-safe bowl. Microwave on high for 6 minutes, remove from microwave and allow to cool. Cover and refrigerate; will remain fresh for several weeks. Makes 1-1/2 cups.

You're invited to A

Spring
Supper
on the
Lawn

Supper on the Lawn

Salmon with Lemon-Parsley Sauce

A flavorful and beautiful dish.

8 4-oz. salmon fillets
1/3 c. mayonnaise
2 T. sweet onion, diced

1 T. fresh parsley, chopped
2 t. lemon juice

Place fillets in a lightly-oiled 13"x9" baking dish. In a small mixing bowl combine remaining ingredients until smooth. Spread evenly over each salmon fillet. Bake at 425 degrees for 15 minutes.

A Shaker-style pegboard hung above a dry sink is the perfect spot for hanging your garden tools.

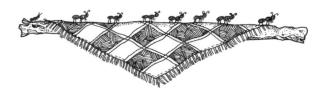

Fresh Lemon Pasta & Basil Sauce

There's nothing like the taste of freshly made pasta.

3 c. all-purpose flour
3 eggs
1/2 t. salt

1/3 c. lemon juice
1 T. oil
2 T. butter

Place flour, eggs and salt in a food processor, pulse until thoroughly combined. Continue to pulse ingredients while adding lemon juice and oil. When dough begins to form, remove from processor and pat into a ball. Cover and allow to rest 20 minutes. Divide dough into quarters. On a lightly floured surface, roll each section of dough into a rectangular shape, 1/8-inch thick. Using a sharp knife or pizza cutter, cut dough into 1/4-inch strips, separate noodles and allow to dry 45 minutes to one hour. Fill a large stockpot with 6 quarts of water and bring to a boil, add pasta. Bring water to a boil again and cook noodles 10 to 15 minutes or until tender. Drain noodles and toss with butter. Serve with Basil Sauce.

Basil Sauce:

4 fresh tomatoes, chopped
1/2 c. green onion, chopped
1/2 c. green pepper, chopped
1/3 c. fresh basil, chopped

1/4 c. fresh cilantro,
2 t. oil
1 t. white vinegar
1 clove garlic, minced

In a large bowl with a tight-fitting lid, combine all ingredients and stir until thoroughly combined. Cover bowl with lid and allow flavors to blend one hour. Stir sauce to redistribute flavors before serving. Refrigerate any leftovers.

Supper on the Lawn

Honey Ham Quiche

Try Prosciutto or peppered ham for a different flavor.

2 c. all-purpose flour
1 t. salt
3/4 c. solid shortening
4 T. cold water
1/3 c. sweet yellow onion,
   chopped
1 sweet red pepper, chopped
2 T. butter

7 eggs, lightly beaten
1/3 c. sour cream
1/3 c. milk
3 T. parsley, chopped
4 oz. honey ham, chopped
14-oz. can artichoke hearts,
   chopped
4 oz. Swiss cheese, shredded

In a large bowl, combine flour and salt. Blend in shortening until mixture is crumbly. Sprinkle with water, one tablespoon at a time, if dough is too stiff. Roll dough out thinly and place in a quiche dish. Bake crust for 10 minutes at 450 degrees. Remove from oven and reduce oven temperature to 325 degrees. In a skillet sauté onions and red pepper in butter until tender. In a mixing bowl beat eggs, sour cream and milk thoroughly. Add parsley, ham and artichoke hearts. Pour over crust and sprinkle cheese over top. Bake until quiche filling is firm. Allow to stand 5 minutes, cut into wedges.

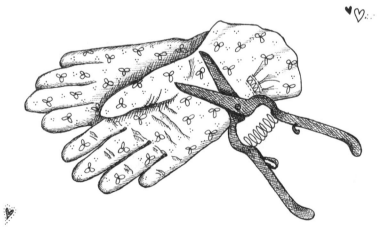

There can be no other occupation like gardening in which, were you to creep up behind someone at their work, you would find them smiling.

-Mirabel Osler

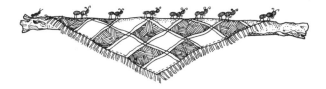

Asparagus & Savory Cream Sauce

When your garden is full of asparagus, it's a sure sign of spring!

1-1/2 lbs. fresh asparagus	1 c. half-and-half
1 T. butter	1/2 c. Swiss cheese, shredded
1 T. all-purpose flour	2 T. butter crackers, crushed

In a non-stick skillet, cook asparagus in very little water until just tender. Drain and place in an oiled 2-quart baking dish. Melt butter in a saucepan, add flour and cook one minute. Pour in half-and-half, whisking to blend with flour. Bring to a boil and cook 2 minutes, constantly stirring. Remove from heat and add cheese. Blend until cheese has melted, pour over asparagus; sprinkle cracker crumbs over top. Place under broiler for 3 minutes until very lightly golden. Serves 4.

Add a little special charm to your party. Play some soft jazz music, dress up your porch with ferns, garden sculptures and urns. Chill beverages in a clean plastic-lined birdbath filled with ice and use miniature instrument ornaments as napkin rings.

Supper on the Lawn

Lemon-Dill Pea Salad

Creamy and delicious!

8-oz. carton of sour cream
1 T. lemon juice
1 green onion, chopped

2 t. sugar
1 t. dill weed
2 c. fresh peas, shelled

Combine sour cream, lemon juice, green onion, sugar and dill weed; blend well. Using a steamer, steam peas until tender, rinse and cool. Fold into sour cream mixture, blend and refrigerate until serving time.

Create a special garden for your favorite feline! "Chester's Garden", could be a half-barrel full of catnip, cat-grass, cat-mint and pussy toes!

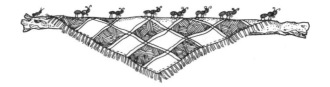

Crisp Vegetables & Ginger Vinaigrette

Garnish serving plates with fresh herb sprigs from your garden.

1/2 lb. fresh green beans
1/2 lb. fresh asparagus spears
3 carrots, cut diagonally
1 lb. zucchini, sliced
1 lb. summer squash, sliced

8 Italian tomatoes, quartered
4-oz. pkg. fresh mushrooms, sliced
1/4 c. oil

Thoroughly wash and rinse all vegetables. Blanch green beans, asparagus and carrots in a large stockpot of boiling water. Drain and set aside. Brush zucchini and squash with oil and grill over medium heat until tender. Set aside to cool slightly. In a large serving bowl, combine all vegetables. Serve with Ginger Vinaigrette on the side.

Ginger Vinaigrette:

1/2 c. white vinegar
2 T. ginger, chopped
1/2 c. cocktail vegetable juice
1/4 c. orange juice

1 t. chives, minced
1/4 t. garlic powder
1 c. oil

Combine vinegar and ginger in a saucepan over medium heat. Bring to a boil and then cool to room temperature. Combine all ingredients, except oil, in a blender and process. As vinaigrette blends, slowly add oil.

Purchase foam wreath forms in a size larger than your dinner plates. Cover the forms with glue and roll in potpourri. When dry, place under each guest's plate. Attach a small bouquet of dried flowers to each napkin, secure with lacy ribbon. As guests leave, offer the wreath as their take-home favor.

Supper on the Lawn

Dilly Onion Bread

An easy-to-make quick bread that's full of flavor!

3 c. all-purpose flour
1/2 c. plus 2 T. sugar
1-1/2 T. baking powder
2/3 c. butter

1 c. milk
4 eggs
5 t. dill seed
2 t. dried, minced onion

Oil 4 6-inch loaf pans; set aside. Using a large bowl, combine flour, sugar and baking powder well; cut in butter. In a separate bowl blend milk, eggs, dill seed and onion. Add to flour mixture and stir. Pour equal amounts into prepared loaf pans and bake at 350 degrees for 30 minutes or until a knife inserted in the center comes out clean. Cool on a rack and serve warm.

A child's red wagon looks lovely filled with pots of white petunias, red geraniums and yellow marigolds.

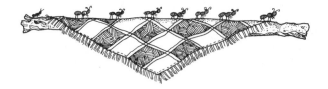

Dreamy Orange Chiffon Cake

A light-textured cake with a delicate orange flavor.

1 medium orange
2 c. all-purpose flour
1-1/2 c. sugar
1 T. baking powder
1 t. salt

1/2 c. oil
5 eggs, separated
3/4 c. water
1 t. vanilla
1/2 t. cream of tartar

Grate rind from orange; set aside. Combine flour, sugar, baking powder and salt in a large mixing bowl. Using a mixer, gradually pour in oil. Add egg yolks, water, vanilla and orange rind. In another mixing bowl, beat egg whites until peaks form, add the cream of tartar. When egg whites are stiff, fold into flour mixture, combine thoroughly and pour into a lightly oiled 10-inch tube pan. Bake at 325 degrees for one hour, or until a cake tester inserted in the middle comes out clean. Cool and remove from pan.

If your gathering is in autumn, stack baskets and wooden crates on your porch. Load them with miniature pumpkins, gourds, mums, pomegranates and sprays of autumn leaves!

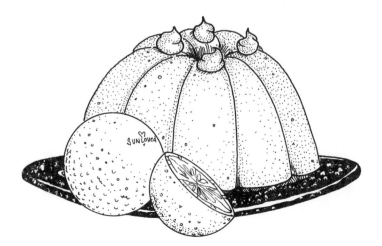

Supper on the Lawn

Rhubarb Torte

Serve with a scoop of French vanilla ice cream on the side.

1 c. all-purpose flour	2 eggs
5 T. powdered sugar	1-1/2 c. sugar
1/8 t. salt	3/4 t. baking powder
1 stick butter	1 lb. fresh rhubarb

In a large bowl combine 3/4 cup flour, powdered sugar and salt. Cut in butter until crumbly. Using hands, shape dough into a ball then spread into the bottom of a 10"x6" baking dish. Bake at 375 degrees for 10 minutes. In another bowl, beat eggs and sugar well. Sift 1/4 cup flour and baking powder together, blend into egg mixture. Add rhubarb and pour over baked crust. Bake for another 30 minutes. Cool slightly before serving.

Leave a clever note so friends can find you when you're working in the garden. Fill a spare gardening glove with fiberfill and stitch closed. Use a fabric marker and write "In the garden" in the middle of the glove, attach a loop to the back and hang on your door. Decorate it with flowers, or write the names of herbs on each finger of the glove!

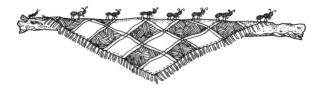

Summer Sparkle

Serve in tall fluted glasses with lots of ice.

48-oz. bottle ruby red grapefruit
   juice
12-oz. can orange juice concentrate, thawed
6 oz. lemonade concentrate,
   thawed

2 lt. bottle lemon-lime soda
Garnish: orange and lemon
   slices

Combine grapefruit juice, orange juice concentrate and lemonade
concentrate in a gallon pitcher. Stir ingredients, cover and refrigerate
until chilled. When ready to serve, add soda to pitcher, stir. Pour into
tall glasses with ice, garnish with orange and lemon slices.

*Take time to enjoy an old-
fashioned game of
horseshoes. If you don't
have horseshoes available,
make circles from old pieces
of roping. Toss them over an
old dowel or stick you've
tapped into the yard. You
might want to make the
circles larger for the
younger children.*

Lavender Sheaf

Perfect for a centerpiece or accent, with a delicate aroma. Easy to assemble, just gather an armful of dried lavender, a couple strands of raffia and 18 inches of 2-inch wide cotton ribbon in your favorite color.

Gather together the lavender until you have a bunch that is 2 or 3 inches in diameter. Tie the bundle together with the raffia and trim off the strands. Using one hand, hold the lavender bundle just under the buds. With your other hand, gently turn the individual lavender stalks clockwise. When you have a design you like, secure the raffia to the bundle with a hot glue gun.

Gently pull on the individual stalks to vary the height and make your sheaf interesting. Trim the bottoms of the lavender evenly so it can stand on its own.

A 1-1/2 inch end should be left on one end of the ribbon, then begin to tie loose knots, spaced evenly, along the length of the ribbon. Place the ribbon over the raffia and glue in place, tucking in or cutting off any extra ribbon.

Do you have a collection of old tins? They make a terrific centerpiece! Fill them with goodies…peppermint sticks, candy corn, jelly beans or dried flowers.

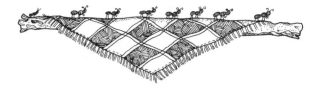

Fragrant Herbal Tier

Decorate your porch with these fragrant accents!

6" dia. terra cotta bulb pan
9" dia. terra cotta bulb pan
12" dia. terra cotta bulb pan
5" terra cotta flowerpot
4" terra cotta flower pot

soil
12 4" potted herb plants
1 rosemary plant
20" grapevine
floral wire

Soak terra cotta pots in water long enough for them to absorb as much as possible. This will let your plants take in the water they need, instead of the pots. Create your first tier by placing the 5-inch flowerpot upside down in the middle of the 12-inch bulb pan. Fill around the flowerpot with potting soil and tuck in 4 of your herb plants spacing them evenly. Fill in with more soil if needed and gently tap the plants in place. Place your smaller flowerpot upside down in the 9-inch bulb pan and fill the flowerpot with soil and 4 herbs also.

Plant the rosemary in the remaining 6-inch bulb pan; set aside. If your grapevine isn't fresh and pliable, soak it in warm water until you're able to easily bend it. Bend the grapevine into overlapping circles forming a ball, secure the ends with floral wire. Gently place the grapevine ball into the center of the rosemary plant, weaving the rosemary through the grapevine.

Create your tier by stacking the bulb pans; largest on the bottom to smallest on the top. The upside down flowerpots in the center of each one will serve as dividers. Remember to water your herbal tier every few days because it will dry out quickly. Snip your herbs and enjoy!

Morning Glory Topiary

This makes a beautiful party favor or hostess gift.

plastic zipping bag
5" painted flowerpot
potting soil
12" trellis or wire form

packet of morning glory seeds
tissue paper
narrow satin ribbon or raffia

Place the plastic zipping bag into the flowerpot and fill with soil; close tightly. Tuck the trellis and seed packet inside the flowerpot. Set the flowerpot in the center of several sheets of tissue paper and gather it up and around the flowerpot. Tie closed with a length of ribbon or raffia formed into a bow.

Attach a gift card with the following instructions:

Empty soil packet into the flowerpot; place the trellis in the center of the soil. Sprinkle on 3 or 4 morning glory seeds and cover with 1/4 inch of soil. Water well and wait for seedlings to emerge. Train them along the trellis as they begin to grow and twine upward.

Grapes, melon balls, watermelon, fresh pineapple, peaches and kiwi look lovely served in a tall stemmed glass topped with a mint sprig.

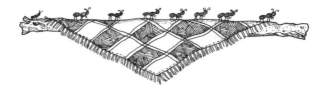

Nasturtium Ice Cubes

These are so beautiful floating in a punch bowl or in tall glasses; they look magical! Simply gather a large bunch of nasturtium blossoms and leaves, wash them well and blot dry.

Fill ice cube trays half-full of water, float nasturtium petals and leaves on top. Place the trays in the freezer, on a level surface, and freeze until solid. Remove trays from the freezer, place more petals and leaves on top, cover with a teaspoon of water; just enough to anchor the petals, but not completely filling each compartment. Refreeze again. Remove trays from freezer and fill with water; freeze overnight. When ready to serve punch, remove ice cubes from trays and place in punch bowl.

Experiment with different types of edible flowers such as pansies, rose petals, rosemary sprigs, or red sage flowers.

Supper on the Lawn

Sunflower & Ivy Table Garland

Try using sunflowers right from your garden.

roll of twisted craft paper
paddle of craft wire

fresh ivy
sunflowers

Measure the twisted craft paper around the edge of your table adding a little extra so it overlaps creating a circle. Wrap wire around the overlapping edges to secure them together. Because the wire will be used to bind the ivy and sunflowers around the craft paper in a continuous circle, don't cut it from the paddle. Place 2 or 3 stems of ivy on the paper circle and secure them in place with wire. Continue to add ivy until the entire circle is covered.

The sunflowers will look their best if kept in cool water until it's time to add them to the garland. When ready to place, trim the sunflowers, leaving one inch of stem attached. Tuck the sunflowers between the ivy stems at equal distances around the garland. Mist them with water to keep them fresh before your guests arrive. If you've used sunflowers from your own garden you can also add a beautiful trailing spray to your garland. Create a pretty bouquet of sunflowers and wire it to the front of your garland; beautiful!

Make your spring supper romantic...decorate with lots of roses and candlelight! Fill a squeeze bottle with fudge sauce and write a romantic message on the outer edge of an extra large dinner plate. Place your dessert in the middle, wonderful!

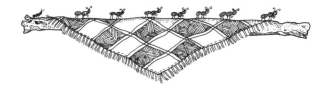

Pressed Flower Placecards

Remember to dry your flowers well in advance.

variety of flowers and leaves
blotting paper
3"x6" blank cards

toothpicks
craft glue
clear self-adhesive film

To make your placecards as pretty as just-picked flowers, harvest your flowers while they're at their prime. Good flower choices for pressing are dusty miller, ferns, Queen Anne's lace, Johnny-jump-ups, pansies, violets, cosmos, impatiens, larkspur and hydrangea. Arrange them on a sheet of blotting paper, then top with another sheet of blotting paper. Place the sheets between heavy books and allow them to dry. You'll need to check them often, some flowers dry in 2 or 3 days while others may take up to 3 weeks. When the flowers are completely dry you can begin to make your placecards.

Fold the blank cards in half lengthwise so they will stand upright and write your guests' names on the front of each card. Arrange your pressed flowers and leaves on the card by dipping the tip of a toothpick in glue. Gently place a small amount of glue on the edges of your flowers and place on your card. When the glue is dry, cut a piece of self-adhesive film slightly larger than the front of your card. Peel the backing from the film and carefully set in place. Trim edges if needed.

Supper on the Lawn

Lily & Mint Baskets

A soft accent that's perfect for a formal supper.

1 small head of cauliflower
1 head of broccoli
dried garlic
stub wires
florist's foam

rectangular wicker basket
florist's adhesive tape
white lilies
white roses
variegated mint sprigs

Trim cauliflower and broccoli into flowerets; set aside. Cut stub wires in half and thread through the base of each floweret, twisting ends of wires together. Wire dried garlic heads also.

Place the florist's foam in cool water until thoroughly soaked, cut to fit basket. Secure tape to basket using strips of florist's tape. Position broccoli, cauliflower and garlic around the outer edges of the basket, hiding the foam. Put lilies in the center of the basket, and trim roses so they will fit nicely in the middle. Tuck in sprigs of mint to fill in any gaps.

How softly runs the after-noon beneath the billowy clouds of June.

-Charles Hanson Towne

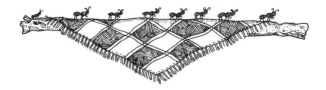

Trellis Ideas

If you have sweet peas, nasturtiums, or morning glories in your garden, try one of these unique trellis ideas!

Window Guards:

Discarded window guards often have ornate detailing and make a beautiful, more formal support for your flowers. Attach it to your wall with a shoulder hook at each side.

Freshly-Cut Branches:

You can make your own rustic trellis using both straight and curved branches. Choose branches that are still green and freshly cut so they can be shaped easily. Create your design and secure the branches with small nails or wire.

Wooden Ladders:

If you have an old barn or know someone who does, you could easily come across a wooden ladder for free! Check out auctions also; ladders that are thought of as no longer useful, can find new life in your garden as a terrific trellis and will really add old-fashioned charm to your garden.

Garden Gates:

Like window guards, the styles of old garden gates can vary from simple to decorative. They're the perfect height for the smaller varieties of sweet peas.

Supper on the Lawn

Fresh Floral May Pole

A miniature version of the traditional May pole.

lady's mantle
pansies
lilies
painted daisies
roses
cosmos

feverfew
3 cylinder-shaped florist's foam
   blocks
36" dowel, 1" diameter
paper ribbon
florist's wire paddle

After harvesting your flowers, place them in a tub of cool water to keep them fresh until you're ready to use them. Mark the center of the foam cylinders and gently slide over the dowel rod. Remove foam from rod and thoroughly soak in cool water. Slide blocks over dowel and gently push to the end, this will become the top of your May pole. Wrap wire beneath the last foam block to keep it from slipping.

Beginning at the top, gently push lady's mantle stems into the foam and form a mound shape. Remove flowers from water as you need them, cutting the stems short. Below the lady's mantle, insert the pansies creating a circle around the foam. Continue with the remaining flowers until the foam is covered. Cut 12 strips of paper ribbon long enough to reach the bottom of the dowel. Hold ribbon against the dowel just below the foam block; secure with wire. Trim if needed so they will blow in the breeze. Place your May pole directly in the garden, or tuck it in a barrel of flowers.

Use chipped or mismatched dishes as flowerpots and arrange them on a bench or windowsill.

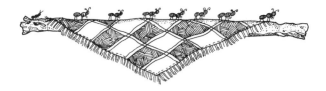

An Herb Garden Right at Your Feet

Walkways made from bricks, flagstones, or slate are perfect spots for herb gardens! In one afternoon you can have a garden at your feet.

The spaces between bricks and pavers are perfect for tucking in thyme plants. Thyme is hardy and has a long blooming season. There are so many varieties to choose from; lemon, silver and variegated, and they release a wonderful fragrance as you step on them. Among the thyme you can plant clumps of variegated sage, parsley, basil, or chives; which will give you a variety of fragrance and texture.

If you'd like, you can continue your herbal path right onto your patio. Simply loosen a few patio stones and remove them. Break up the soil and add some compost. Plant the herbs around the edges of your patio or in a decorative pattern.

Create a cutting garden this year. Grow flowers that are known for long-lasting blooms such as zinnia, cosmos, larkspur, black-eyed Susan and daisies.

Supper on the Lawn

Garden Lighting

As your guests linger to visit, enhance the beauty of your garden with lighting.

Small white lights outlining a gazebo or arbor are beautiful, or wrap a strand around a grapevine wreath for a dazzling window accent.

Tuck a votive candle inside an old railroad lantern then hang it from a garden hook.

Place votives or tea lights in tiny terra cotta pots filled with sand. Place them along a garden path or walkway.

Floating candles are lovely when you place them in a bird bath.

Group pillar candles in large sand-filled terra cotta pots, or create a hurricane light by placing a glass chimney in a sand-filled terra cotta pot.

Minnow buckets become beautiful luminarias when you place a votive inside.

Fallen tree branches add a rustic look when filled with votives. Clamp the branch securely and using a spade drill bit, drill an opening large enough to tuck in a tea light. Peel the outer layers of bark from around the holes to prevent it from becoming a fire hazard.

Create a lovely centerpiece! Soak florist's foam in water then place in a plastic container. Cover the foam with sheet moss and tuck in your favorite flowers.

Candlelight Dinner
on the porch

Creamy Wild Rice Soup

Terrific served with warm pumpernickel bread and herb butter.

4-1/2 c. fresh mushrooms, sliced
1 c. sweet onion, chopped
1 c. celery, chopped
4 T. butter
1/2 c. flour

4 c. chicken broth
1 c. half-and-half
1-1/2 c. wild rice, cooked
1 T. fresh marjoram
salt and pepper to taste

Combine mushrooms, onion and celery with butter in a Dutch oven.
Cook over medium heat until vegetables are tender. Sprinkle flour over
vegetables, stirring well. Add broth and simmer until thick. Reduce
heat and add half-and-half, rice, marjoram, salt and pepper. Continue
to cook over low heat until thoroughly heated. Serves 6.

Menu
Soup du Jour
Wild Rice

*Punch drainage holes in watering can bottoms, add dirt and fill with petunias
or geraniums. Stagger them on your porch steps for a welcome look.*

Herb-Seasoned Spinach Puffs

Add a spicy mustard sauce for dipping.

2 10-oz. pkgs. frozen chopped
   spinach, thawed & drained
2 c. herb-seasoned stuffing mix

1 c. Parmesan cheese, grated
6 eggs, lightly beaten
1/3 c. butter, softened

Drain and squeeze spinach until all liquid is removed. Combine with stuffing mix, cheese, eggs and butter, mixing well. Form into 2-inch balls and place on a lightly oiled baking sheet. Cover with foil and chill overnight. Bake at 350 degrees for 15 minutes or until heated throughout. Place on paper towels to absorb excess liquids.

Dried roses from a special occasion can be gathered in a moss-covered basket as a keepsake.

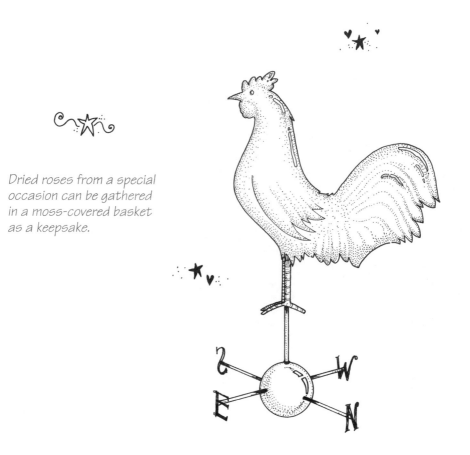

Dinner on the Porch

Peppered Beef in Parsley Crust

Serve thinly sliced with creamy horseradish on the side.

2 T. whole peppercorns
4 T. butter, softened

1 c. parsley, chopped
2 lb. tenderloin roast

Grind peppercorns until coarse in texture and spread evenly on a large platter. In a small mixing bowl, blend butter and parsley well. Spread butter mixture over roast, covering all sides evenly. Place roast on platter and roll in cracked peppercorns until roast is coated. Bake at 425 degrees for one hour or until meat thermometer registers 135 degrees, this will produce a rare roast. Let rest before carving.

Fashion romantic garlands to hang on the porch swing, over the door, or across the buffet table.

Melon Salad with Honey Dressing

Beautiful served in a crystal bowl.

1 cantaloupe melon
1 honeydew melon
3 T. lime juice
2 T. balsamic vinegar

3 T. honey
2 c. baby bibb lettuce
2 c. arugula

Slice melons in half, peel and cut into chunks. In a small bowl. mix lime juice, vinegar and honey together, blending well. Pour over melon and toss. Place torn lettuce and arugula on salad plates. Using a slotted spoon, remove melon from bowl and place on lettuce, drizzle dressing over top. Serves 4.

If you have a heat wave this summer, enjoy an evening supper under the shade of old trees, on the porch, or in a gazebo.

Dinner on the Porch

Spinach & Cheese Stuffed Chicken Breasts

Try this dish served over wild rice.

6 5-oz. skinless, boneless
  chicken breasts
1/4 c. oil
2 T. thyme, dried and crushed
2 T. butter
1/4 c. sweet onion, diced

14-oz. pkg. frozen spinach,
  thawed
1/2 c. cottage cheese
1/4 c. Parmesan cheese
1/2 t. basil

Brush chicken breasts with oil, sprinkle on thyme and set aside. Melt butter in a saucepan and sauté onion until tender. Remove from heat and set aside. Squeeze all liquid from spinach and combine in a large mixing bowl with cottage cheese, Parmesan cheese and basil. Stir in sautéed onions and mix well. Place a portion of the stuffing mixture in center of each chicken breast and bring sides to center, overlapping. Secure with metal skewers and bake at 375 degrees for 30 minutes. Remove skewers before serving. Serves 6.

Crunchy Spinach-Apple Salad

A wonderful salad for a summer evening.

1/4 c. walnuts, chopped
1/2 c. oil
2 T. fruit-flavored vinegar

4 c. spinach leaves, torn
1 tart apple, sliced but not peeled
1 t. lemon juice

Toast walnuts in a baking dish at 350 degrees for 5 minutes; set aside. Combine oil and vinegar in a jar with a tight fitting lid, shake to mix well. Place spinach and apple slices in a large serving bowl; sprinkle with lemon juice. Drizzle with dressing, top with toasted walnuts and toss.

Retreat to the backyard on a crisp Indian Summer evening. Count the chirps that the crickets make...gaze at a full moon...have someone push you on an old tree swing!

Dinner on the Porch

Chive & Dijon Crab Cakes

Moist inside, crunchy outside.

1 lb. fresh crabmeat, flaked
1/2 c. fresh bread crumbs
2 T. fresh parsley
2 T. heavy cream
1 T. lemon juice
2 t. chives, chopped

1 t. Dijon mustard
1/8 t. cayenne pepper
1 large egg
1 large egg yolk
1/3 c. dry bread crumbs
1/2 stick buttter

Combine first 10 ingredients in a large mixing bowl; stir well to blend.
Shape mixture into 8 patties; set aside. Place dry bread crumbs in a
bowl and dip each of the 8 patties in the bread crumbs. Cover both
sides well. Melt butter in a large skillet over medium-high heat. Add
crab cakes and cook 5 minutes or until golden, turning once. Repeat
with remaining crab cakes. Serves 4.

*Make your dinner on the porch romantic.
Set out a small table for two covered with
a lace tablecloth; set a rose bowl in the
middle filled with sweetheart roses. Play
soft music and decorate with candles
everywhere…along the porch steps, railing
and windowsills. If you'd like more privacy, a
wooden screen would be lovely!*

Marinated Sugar Snap Peas

Prepare this dish ahead of time if you need to.

1-1/2 lb. sugar snap peas
1/2 red onion, thinly sliced

1 garlic clove, crushed
1/3 c. olive oil

In a large stockpot, heat enough water to cover peas. Boil until crisp-tender, approximately one minute. Drain and rinse with cool water. Place in a large mixing bowl with remaining ingredients; gently toss. Cover and refrigerate 30 minutes. When ready to serve, remove from refrigerator and allow to come to room temperature. Serves 8.

Invite a group of friends over for swapping seeds and plant cuttings! Make your invitations from empty seed packets... just tuck a garden marker inside with the date and time of your party. Ask each friend to bring some seeds or cuttings from her garden, along with notes on how to care for them. Serve simple finger foods and refreshing punch. Give each guest a small terra cotta pot with a cutting from your own garden as a favor to take home!

Dinner on the Porch

Herb Garden Bread

Enjoy this warm from the oven with real butter.

3 to 4 c. bread flour
3 T. sugar
2 pkgs. active dry yeast
1-1/2 t. salt
1/4 t. marjoram, dried and
   crushed

1/4 t. thyme, dried and crushed
1/2 c. water
1/4 c. milk
1/4 c. plus 1 T. butter
1 egg

Combine 1-1/2 cups flour, sugar, yeast, salt, marjoram and thyme in a large mixing bowl. In a small saucepan, mix water, milk and 1/4 cup butter, heating until warm. Add to flour mixture and combine well. Add egg and enough of the remaining flour to make a soft dough. Knead 5 minutes on a lightly floured surface, adding more flour if needed to make dough smooth. Oil the inside of a large bowl and place dough inside; turning to coat. Cover and allow to rise until double in size. Punch down dough, and place on a lightly floured surface. Separate dough into 3 sections and allow to rest 10 minutes. Roll each of the 3 sections into a 30-inch rope; braid ropes together. Form into a circle, pinching ends together to seal, and place on an oiled baking sheet. Allow to rise until double in bulk. Bake 30 minutes at 375 degrees, covering with foil if necessary to prevent overbrowning. Remove from oven, brush with remaining butter and allow to cool slightly before slicing.

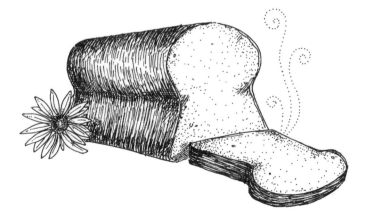

Tie a tiny herbal wreath around the neck of a bottle of sparkling water.

Savory Butters

Try these wonderful butters on hot corn on the cob or still warm homemade bread.

Parsley Butter

1/2 c. butter, softened
1 garlic clove, minced

1 t. fresh parsley, chopped
2 t. lemon peel, grated

Combine all ingredients in a small crock, blending until smooth. Keeps fresh in the refrigerator for 2 weeks.

Peppercorn Butter

1 c. butter, softened

3/4 t. ground black pepper

Blend ingredients together, beating until fluffy.

Fines Herbes Butter

1/2 c. parsley, chopped
1/4 c. chives, chopped

3 tarragon leaves, chopped
1/2 c. butter

Mix herbs well. Add one teaspoon to butter, blending well. Add more herb blend if desired.

Dost thou love life? Then waste not time, for time is the stuff that life is made of.
-Benjamin Franklin

Dinner on the Porch

Creamy Herbed New Potatoes

A new version of scalloped potatoes...terrific!

2 T. butter
1/2 lb. new potatoes, sliced thin
1 T. all-purpose flour

2 t. fresh sage, chopped
1/4 c. Stilton or Feta cheese
2/3 c. half-and-half

Butter the inside of a 13"x9" baking dish. Using one-third of the remaining ingredients, layer potato slices, sprinkle on flour, sage, cheese and half-and-half. Repeat layering 2 more times, dot top with remaining butter. Bake at 350 degrees for 1-1/2 hours or until golden brown. Serves 2.

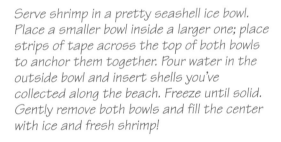

Serve shrimp in a pretty seashell ice bowl. Place a smaller bowl inside a larger one; place strips of tape across the top of both bowls to anchor them together. Pour water in the outside bowl and insert shells you've collected along the beach. Freeze until solid. Gently remove both bowls and fill the center with ice and fresh shrimp!

Chocolate Angel Food Cake

Garnish with a few strawberry slices...wonderful!

3/4 c. cake flour, sifted
4 T. unsweetened cocoa
1-1/4 c. sugar
10 large egg whites, room
    temperature

1/4 t. salt
1 t. cream of tartar
1 t. vanilla
1 pt. strawberries
sugar to taste

Combine flour, cocoa and sugar in a large mixing bowl until thoroughly blended. In a separate bowl, beat egg whites just until peaks form. Blend in salt and cream of tartar. Beat until stiff, then fold in vanilla. Blend flour mixture into egg whites a spoonful at a time, mixing gently after each addition. Place batter in a 10-inch angel food cake pan, and bake at 350 degrees for 40 minutes, or until cake is browned. Allow air to circulate around cake pan by slipping the hole over the neck of a weighted bottle. The cake should cool completely in this position. When cooled, remove from pan and place on a cake plate. Combine strawberries with sugar and serve with cake slices.

Dinner on the Porch

Raspberry & Citrus Punch

Refreshing!

12-oz. can frozen lemonade
   concentrate, thawed
3 c. water
1/2 gal. raspberry sherbet

48 oz. lemon-lime soda, chilled
Garnish: fresh raspberries and
   lemon, thinly sliced

Combine lemonade concentrate with water, mixing well and pour into a punch bowl. Using an ice-cream scoop drop sherbet into lemonade mixture. Add soda, stir to blend. Float lemon slices and raspberries in punch for garnish.

Rather than covering your fireplace with a fireboard this summer, try filling it with a basket of dried statice, roses, hydrangea and yarrow.

Lavender Bird Cage

A unique accent that gives off a soft fragrance as the evening breezes drift by. Begin by choosing fresh lavender blossoms; they will need to be flexible enough for you to bend. Using 2 wreath forms of the same size, cover both completely with lavender. Lay several lavender stems on the form and tightly wrap with nylon cord. Continue to layer the stems, overlapping them to hide the wreath form. When you have completely covered the form, tie the nylon cord securely. Repeat with the remaining wreath form.

Place one wreath inside the other, forming a cage, and wire them together tightly at the top and bottom. Place several lengths of narrow satin ribbon through the opening of the wreaths and tie into a loose bow; allow the ribbon ends to fall loosely. Attach loops of ribbon at the top of the wreaths to serve as a hanger.

If you'd like you can add flowers or an abandoned bird's nest inside your "cage" as decoration.

To dig and delve in nice clean dirt can do a mortal little hurt.
-John Kendrick Bangs

Dinner on the Porch

Wicker...the Look of Yesteryear

Turn your porch into a full-fledged outdoor room! Furnish it with a pair of wicker rockers or settee, add some plump cushions you can sink into and you have the perfect companions for a cozy porch corner.

Wicker has a wonderful time-worn feeling and a simple presence...it seems to get better with age. It does; however, take a little extra special care to keep it looking good.

Dust your wicker furniture and cushions occasionally with the brush attachment on your vacuum. Clean it as needed, using a mild detergent or oil soap and warm water. Rinse any soap residue off completely and allow it to air-dry, or gently wipe the piece dry before replacing your cushions.

If your wicker is antique, you can enjoy it outdoors as long as it's on a covered porch. To keep the glued joints from loosening in the cold weather, be sure to bring it indoors or store it in a heated area.

Wicker comes in a variety of styles...weathered, antique and new; and has been loved for over a century. If you don't have wicker, try it; what better way to introduce a sense of the past to your home.

Rose Bud & Pearl Garland

This is simply beautiful. For a romantic touch, arrange it across the length of your table, winding it around your candles and centerpiece. To make one 24-inch garland you'll need 32 inches of strong thread, one cup of whole dried rosebuds, one small needle with a large eye and 36 faux pearls.

Tie a loop at the end of your thread if you want to hang your garland. If you want to let it wind the length of your table, simply tie a knot at the end; trimming any excess. Thread the string on the needle and push the needle through the center of a rosebud, sliding it to the end of the string. Add a pearl and slide it next to the rosebud. Repeat until you reach the end of your string. Remove the needle and tie a knot in the end, or a loop for hanging.

A bouquet of yarrow, roses, hydrangea, larkspur and grasses gathered from the fields is perfect for a country-style centerpiece.

Dinner on the Porch

Wax-Preserved Flowers

Flowers from your garden make beautiful additions to gifts and table settings. Depending on the variety, you can preserve their beauty for several days to many weeks using paraffin wax as a preservative.

Begin by removing all the leaves from your flowers, then cool them in the refrigerator for one hour.

Using caution, melt 4 pounds of paraffin, found in the canning section of most grocery stores, over low heat in a double boiler. (Caution: because wax is flammable, a double boiler must be used.)

When the wax has melted, remove the double boiler from the heat and stir in 2-1/2 cups of mineral oil. Using a candy thermometer, allow the mixture to cool to a temperature of 130 degrees, wax that is too hot will burn the flowers.

Using tweezers, carefully dip the refrigerated flowers, one at a time, in the wax. Turn the flower to coat all petals, allow any excess to drip off. Immediately plunge the flower into a bowl of ice water for 15 minutes, allowing the wax to cool and set. Remove from ice water and set on wax paper. Repeat with remaining flowers. When all flowers have been waxed, allow the paraffin to cool until solid; then discard.

Experiment with different flowers to see what works best for you, some will last only several days, others several months.

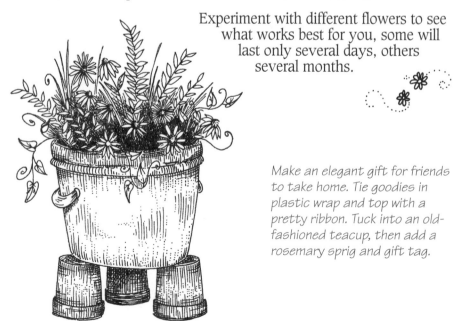

Make an elegant gift for friends to take home. Tie goodies in plastic wrap and top with a pretty ribbon. Tuck into an old-fashioned teacup, then add a rosemary sprig and gift tag.

Potpourri Picture Frame

Using leftover petals, ribbon and flower buds, you can create a beautiful picture frame. You'll need a wooden or plastic picture frame that's one-inch wide on the front, green sphagnum moss, German statice, dried flowers and herbs, and raffia or ribbon strands.

If your frame has a glossy finish, you'll need to dull it with a piece of 100 grit sandpaper. Using a low-temperature glue gun, attach the moss around the frame; covering the edges and front completely. Glue German statice on top of the moss to serve as a filler. Using pieces of dried flowers such as larkspur, baby's breath, pepper berries, or rose buds glue them around the frame as desired. You may want to group your flowers into small bunches and create small clusters around the frame. Fill in any bare areas with some sweet Annie or ferns.

Drape your ribbon or raffia around the frame, tucking it around and behind flowers if needed. Glue in place. Allow to dry completely then insert your picture.

A morning glory at my window satisfies me more than the metaphysics of books.
-Walt Whitman

Friendly Flowers Pass the hours

Dinner on the Porch

Garden Accents

Simple accents can give your garden an old-fashioned, romantic feeling. Create a cottage garden with jumbles of flowers, climbing roses and vines, herbs by the kitchen door and paths made from cobbles or bricks. Place a bench outside your door for enjoying the garden when the weather allows.

In the past, gates and doors kept farm animals out of the garden. They still serve this purpose today; however they are a part of garden decorating as well. According to an old custom, many people hang a horseshoe over their garden door or gate to bring good luck to the household; just remember to hang it with the opening on the top so the luck doesn't run out!

Arches are a lovely way to add a feeling of times past. Build a rustic arch around your doorway and cover it with roses, clematis, wisteria, or trumpet vine to give a wonderful informal feeling. Keep the door a simple color to allow the flowers to really show through.

But don't go into Mr. McGregor's garden!
-Beatrix Potter

Refreshing Bath Salts

A bath salt with fizz!

1/2 c. baking soda
1/4 c. citric acid
1/4 c. cornstarch

3/4 t. fragrance oil
2 drops food coloring

Combine all ingredients; mixing well to distribute the oil thoroughly. Try different types of fragrance oil such as lemon, lavender, hyacinth, mint, or gardenia. For gift-giving, pour into old-fashioned canning jars and top with a raffia bow. Tuck in a note that says, "Sprinkle 2 tablespoons of herbal bath salts in bath water for a refreshing, relaxing bath."

To own a bit of ground, to scratch it with a hoe, to plant seeds, and watch the renewal of life, this is the commonest delight of the race, the most satisfactory thing a man can do.
-Charles Dudley Warner

Dinner on the Porch

Herbal Finger Towels

For an elegant addition to your candlelight dinner, offer your guests these easy-to-make fragrant finger towels. In warm water, rinse colorful, clean washcloths. Wring out any excess water. In the center of each towel, place scented geranium leaves, lemon balm leaves or lavender buds. Fold and roll each washcloth. Place on a microwave-safe plate and heat for 2 minutes on high. Remove from the microwave and place on a decorative tray or platter with a pair of tongs on the side.

After dinner, pass the tray to your guests, letting them choose a wash-cloth; empty the herbs onto another tray.

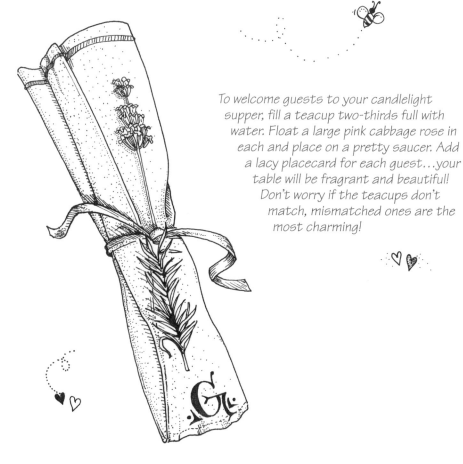

To welcome guests to your candlelight supper, fill a teacup two-thirds full with water. Float a large pink cabbage rose in each and place on a pretty saucer. Add a lacy placecard for each guest...your table will be fragrant and beautiful! Don't worry if the teacups don't match, mismatched ones are the most charming!

Join us for a little

Child's

Play

Child's Play

Stuffed Pockets

 Easy for little hands to hold on to!

4 slices bacon
3 whole pitas, cut in half
lettuce leaves
6 slices ham, thinly sliced

6 slices Cheddar cheese
1 red onion, sliced into rings
1 tomato, sliced
ranch-style salad dressing

Fry bacon until crisp and lay on paper towels to drain. Crumble and set aside. Slightly open pita halves and layer lettuce, ham, cheese, onion and tomato inside. Top with salad dressing and crumbled bacon.

Begin a tradition of Family Night in your home. Choose one night each week your family can spend time together. Take a walk and learn about nature, read a story, or lend a hand to an elderly neighbor.

Zoo-Pendous Sandwiches

Shaped like all the animals your kids love!

4 oz. cream cheese, softened
8-oz. pkg. Cheddar cheese,
   shredded

1/4 c. mayonnaise
1 loaf firm white bread

Place cream cheese, Cheddar cheese and mayonnaise in a food processor and pulse until thoroughly combined. Place cheese spread on bread slices to make sandwiches. Using your favorite animal-shaped cookie cutters, cut sandwiches. Serves 6.

Help your kids create their own rainbow with a garden hose, name all the colors, then cool off with a water fight!

Child's Play

Summer Fruit Sandwiches

Easy-to-eat, open-faced sandwiches.

8-oz. pkg. strawberry cream
    cheese, softened
10 slices pound cake

10 strawberries, sliced
3 bananas, sliced
seedless grapes, sliced in half

Spread cream cheese on pound cake slices. Layer fruit on top, gently
pressing into cream cheese mixture.

*Kids will enjoy watching the birds splash around when they make their own
birdbath! Use an old garbage can lid filled with a layer of pebbles to weigh it
down; fill with water. Place it on a tree stump or on a pedestal. Remember to
fill it with fresh water daily.*

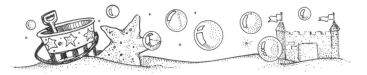

Polka Dot Salad

A colorful, crunchy pasta salad!

1-1/2 c. rigatoni, uncooked
1 cucumber, peeled and chopped
1 c. carrots, chopped
1/2 c. radishes, thinly sliced
1/4 c. red onion, chopped
2 c. cooked ham, cubed

1 T. fresh parsley, chopped
1 c. mayonnaise-style salad
  dressing
1 T. sugar
1 T. vinegar
salt and pepper to taste

Prepare pasta according to package directions, rinse with cool water and set aside to cool. Mix in remaining vegetables and ham. In a small bowl, combine parsley, salad dressing, sugar and vinegar. Blend well and pour over salad ingredients. Toss to combine.

Make an old-fashioned daisy chain, they make pretty crowns for little girls!

Child's Play

Fishin' for Fruit Salad

The kids will have a "whale of a time" with this!

1 watermelon
2 honeydew melons
2 cantaloupe melons
3 qts. strawberries, sliced

3 navel oranges, peeled and
   sliced
1 lb. seedless red grapes
1 lb. seedless green grapes

Using a pencil or marker, make the outline of a whale on the watermelon. Cut slowly and follow the picture below. Using a melon baller, remove the watermelon and place in a large bowl. Using a large spoon, remove any excess watermelon remaining on the inside. Slice the honeydew and cantaloupe melons in half and remove seeds. Using a melon baller, scoop out melon and add to mixing bowl. Add remaining fruit and carefully toss. Fill whale with mixed fruit and refrigerate until serving time. Serves 18.

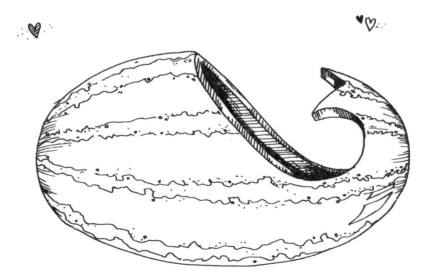

If you'd like for the kids to have a harvest party and aren't near a farm or barn, use a church or school gym, or large basement instead. Decorate with bales of hay, colorful autumn leaves and safe barnyard tools to create a farm scene!

Flowerpot Parfait

Layers of berries and yogurt served in a tiny terra cotta pot!

8-oz. container of berry yogurt
2 c. fresh strawberries, sliced

1 banana, sliced
4 t. granola cereal

Line 4 small terra cotta pots with foil muffin cups. Spoon in ingredients; alternating berries and banana between yogurt. Top with granola.

Visit a "pick-your-own" produce farm. Fresh picked fruits and vegetables can't be beat!

Child's Play

Sunny Snack Mix

Grab a handful...you'll love it as much as the kids!

2 c. raisins
2 c. peanuts
2 c. candy corn

2 c. candy-coated chocolate
    pieces

Combine all ingredients in a large bowl; mix. Serves 16.

Plant some night-blooming flowers such as nicotiania, evening primrose, or moonflowers.

Garden Party Cookies

Pull out all your favorite spring and summer cookie cutters...flowers, watering cans, chicks and birdhouses for these special cookies.

1-1/4 c. sugar
2/3 c. shortening
2 eggs
1 T. milk
1 t. vanilla

3 c. flour, sifted
2 t. baking powder
1 t. salt
1 t. orange peel, grated

Cream together sugar, shortening, eggs, milk and vanilla. In a separate bowl, combine flour, baking powder, salt and orange peel. Blend into sugar mixture. Roll out to 1/4-inch thickness on a lightly floured surface and cut with cookie cutters. Bake at 375 degrees for 8 to 10 minutes. Remove from cookie sheet and allow to cool before icing. Makes 6 or 7 dozen cookies.

Old shoes and old friends
are best.
　　　-Proverb

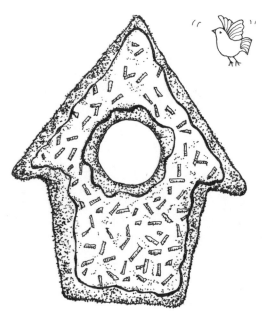

Child's Play

Sunshine Punch

They'll love it...and so easy to make!

2 pkgs. unsweetened fruit-
   flavored drink mix
3-oz. can frozen orange juice
   concentrate

46-oz. can pineapple juice
1 qt. lemon-lime soda, chilled
Garnish: strawberries, pineapple
   chunks, banana slices

Prepare drink mix and orange juice concentrate according to package directions. Combine in a large punch bowl. Add pineapple juice, stir together and chill. Before serving, add lemon-lime soda and mix. Slide fruit onto the bottom half of plastic straws and place into individual glasses, add chilled punch.

The next time you visit the beach, look for a piece of driftwood, empty crab shells, stones, or sand dollars and make a mobile. Use nylon thread to hang them from a piece of driftwood.

Create a Secret Hide-out

Kids love to have secret hiding places, so make them a hide-out to call their very own! To create this "living playhouse" you'll need 6 tall, flexible poles, or tender saplings; willow or birch are good choices. In a prepared garden bed, space them evenly apart in a circle and sink them into the ground about 6 inches deep. Remember to leave room for an entrance!

Bring the tops of the poles or saplings together tee-pee style and secure with heavy twine. Plant quick-growing seeds around the base. Try moonflower, morning glory, scarlet runner beans or sweet peas. As the vines grow, train them to climb the walls of the hide-out. In no time at all they'll have their own "secret garden"!

What was Paradise? But a garden, an orchard of trees and herbs, full of pleasure, and nothing there but delights.
—William Lawson

Child's Play

A Sunflower Playhouse

It's so easy to create this fast-growing playhouse! In a prepared garden bed, mark off a rectangle as large as you'd like the playhouse to be. Along the outside of the rectangle, plant sunflower seeds. Choose one of the tall-growing varieties such as Giant Greystripe or Giant Mammoth. Plant groups of 2 or 3 seeds about 12 inches apart...don't forget to leave a doorway! You can even plant morning glory seeds between the sunflower seeds; they'll fill in any gaps.

As the plants grow, they'll form giant walls with an open ceiling to enjoy the blue sky and summer sun! When the plants are fully grown, the seed heads can be pulled toward the center and secured to form a peaked roof on the playhouse. Once the seeds begin to ripen, you can leave the sunflower seeds for the birds to enjoy... they'll just help themselves!

Play games with your kids this summer! Old favorites such as "I-Spy" or a scavenger hunt are fun, and playing dress-up is always a favorite with little girls.

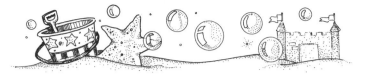

Flower Pockets

A wonderful gift for Grandma or a favorite Aunt, made from fragrant flowers from your garden.

wallpaper
light-weight cardboard
trims such as lace or eyelet

8 to 10 inches of satin ribbon
dried flowers and herbs
floral scented essential oil

Glue wallpaper to cardboard, smoothing out any visible glue lines; let dry. On the cardboard side, draw 2 identical hearts. You can use a cookie cutter or stencil for a pattern if you'd like. Cut out the hearts and glue eyelet or lace on the outer edge of the wallpaper side. On the inside of one heart, glue a length of satin ribbon to serve as a hanger; let dry. Glue the 2 hearts together, leaving the top open. When completely dry, fill the heart with dried flowers and herbs. Add a drop of essential oil.

Watch for meteor showers! The best time is from August 10th to the 13th when you can see an average of 65 meteors light up the sky each hour! It's almost like enjoying fireworks!

Child's Play

A Garden Scrapbook

As the days become longer and the weather becomes warmer, there are so many wonderful changes taking place outdoors. Help your children keep track of them by making a garden scrapbook. A long length of continuous paper can hold lots of sketches, paintings and pictures that show the changes in your garden and yard throughout spring and summer.

When spring arrives, begin the garden scrapbook by having the children cut out a large tree and leaves from construction paper. Using old magazines or catalogs, cut out pictures of spring flowers such as tulips, lilacs, or bleeding-hearts and animals that are born in the spring. As the garden changes with summer, they can add other pictures or drawings too. They can even add dates that are special to them. For example, when did they hear the first bird's song or see the first hummingbird? Did they get out of bed early to see a sunrise or stay up late and see their first shooting star? After new pictures are added, the scrapbook can be rolled up and stored for the next set of pictures or important dates.

At the end of summer look over the scrapbook together as a family and take the opportunity to talk about the changing seasons and what special things happen around us every day.

Kids will love a fun outdoor party with a cowboy theme! Drape a big blanket on the picnic table, serve sandwiches on graniteware plates and wrap the flatware in big squares of burlap tied with roping! Use western boots as vases for summer flowers...just tuck a small vase inside each boot to hold the flowers and water.

The Learning Garden

Children will love creating this garden where they can experiment with nature! In a section of your garden set up a rain gauge, sundial, birdhouse and birdbath. Plant some seeds and track their growth on a chart. Plant zinnias, purple coneflowers, thistles or globe amaranth...flowers that attract butterflies and see how many different butterfly varieties visit your garden.

To make a rain gauge you'll need:

1 wide-mouth funnel
1 wide-mouth canning jar
permanent marker
measuring tapes
1 olive jar, 1" diameter

Place a wide-mouth funnel inside the canning jar. The funnel will prevent some of the rainwater from evaporating before it can be measured. If you get very little rain where you live, measuring a small amount of rainfall in a large jar can be hard; here's how to get a more accurate measurement. Fill the canning jar with one inch of water, then pour it into the olive jar. Using a permanent marker, mark the water level on the outside of the olive jar and divide that inch mark into smaller 1/4-inch measurements. You may have more than one inch of rain, or if you want to see how much rain fell in a week, you'll want to add one or 2 more inch marks on the outside of the olive jar. Set your canning jar outside where it can collect rain and after a rainstorm bring your jar inside. To see how much rain really fell, pour it into the olive jar and check your measurement.

Enjoy an Olympic sports event with the neighborhood kids! Keep the races fun...have kids balance a feather on their head while they carry a water balloon! Make fun award ribbons for all!

Child's Play

Children's Vegetable Garden

Fast growing, fun vegetables are the key to this garden! If you capture kids' interest, they'll be eager to tend their own crops!

Begin by preparing an area with plenty of room for little ones to have fun. Choose seeds that are fun...Tiny Planet carrots are bite-size and round, Easter eggplant looks like a giant goose egg and Cutie Pops Popcorn is a palm-size version of the bigger corn varieties. Choose seeds that are large so they don't get lost easily; squash, cucumbers or beans are good choices for little hands.

Have fun planning the garden before you start. Make a tunnel from sturdy wire for climbers such as gourds or cucumbers. Insert sturdy stakes for tomatoes and pole-beans creating a wall around "their" garden.

Remember to mulch to keep the weeds down, then wait for your bountiful harvest!

Hunt for fossils this summer! If you live near an area with a lot of limestone or sandstone, you'll have a good chance of finding preserved plants or small sea creatures.

For the Birds!

Easy-to-make treats your feathered friends will love!

Tree-top Tarts:

1/2 T. baking soda
1 c. cornmeal
1 c. all-purpose flour
1 c. bread crumbs

3/4 c. raisins
1/2 c. bacon drippings
1/4 t. sand or grit
1 c. water

Combine first 4 ingredients together in a large mixing bowl. Blend in raisins, bacon drippings, grit and water, mixing well. Lightly oil muffin tins or use paper liners, and fill muffin cups two-thirds full. Bake for 15 minutes at 350 degrees. Cool and remove from muffin cups. Place in an open birdfeeder or in a feeder with a tray.

Peanut Butter Balls:

3-1/2 c. oatmeal
4 c. water
1 lb. suet

1-1/2 c. peanut butter
3-1/2 c. cornmeal
3-1/2 c. cream of wheat

Cook oatmeal with water for 2 minutes, stirring often. Add suet and peanut butter, stir until both are melted and well-blended. Add remaining ingredients and stir. Allow to cool slightly. When mixture has cooled enough to handle, shape into balls or logs. Place in an empty open-weave potato sack and hang in a tree, or insert a wreath pin in the top and string a ribbon through it for hanging on a tree. Logs could be placed on a birdfeeder tray.

Child's Play

Summer Garden Art

Did you know you can use the heat and light from the sun to create artwork? Using special light-sensitive paper, found at nature stores and hobby shops, you can make prints of many things in your garden!

Leaves, flowers, herbs and grasses work best because they lie flat. Use your imagination! Choose flowers and leaves that are different shapes and sizes, then arrange them on your paper. Use a piece of clear plexiglass to hold everything down and leave it in the sunlight for 5 minutes.

Remove the plexiglass and carefully lift your objects off the paper. Place your sheet of paper in a tub of warm water for one minute to allow the images to become permanent; let dry. All of your objects will appear white on a blue background!

Be creative with your garden art! Frame them, cut out the designs and glue onto dark paper for notecards, or make a collage of the changing flowers and leaves you find in the garden from spring to autumn.

Celebrate our forefathers by hosting a "Pioneer Day Picnic". Make homemade ice cream, tin-can butter and cook over an open fire. Enjoy a three-legged race, wagon ride and friendly game of horse shoes. End the day with everyone gathered around the campfire recalling stories of earlier ancestors.

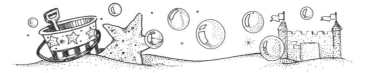

Birds of a Feather...

Will flock to your homemade birdfeeder! A great kids' project because they're so easy to make.

large, empty coffee can
spray paint, variety of colors
1/2-inch thick scrap board
pencil

small finishing nails
dowel rods
wire

Begin by removing the bottom of the coffee can and any labels or stickers on the outside. Slip the can over a long piece of wood and rest it on a saw horse. This allows you to spray paint the can without having to hold onto it. You may want to use several colors to make an abstract design, or be creative and paint a rainbow or American flag pattern on your can. Allow the can to dry completely.

Using scrap wood, measure 2-1/4 inches along the edge and draw a straight line across the length of the wood. Place the edge of your can on the line and draw along the outside of the can; repeat. This will make two semi-circle shapes that you will slip into the ends of your can when it's finished. Using small nails, nail a 2-inch length of dowel into the middle of each semi-circle for a perch. Insert one semi-circle into each end of the open can and nail into place. Drill a hole at the top of each side of the feeder and insert wire for hanging your birdfeeder. Be sure to twist the wire securely and leave the sharp edge resting on top of the feeder pointed away from the opening. This will protect both little hands and the birds.

Have the kids put on an old-fashioned puppet show! Make up your own story or act out a familiar one. Shine a flashlight or table lamp on the puppets...they'll cast a shadow on the wall for the big show!

Child's Play

Make a Weather Vane

A great addition to your learning garden!

thin cardboard
1 plastic straw
white glue
pencil

straight pin
tin can
flat board
modeling clay

Cut 2 triangles the same size from cardboard. Cut slits in the ends of the straw and glue the triangles in place; allow to dry. In the bottom of an empty tin can, drill a hole just large enough for the pencil to fit into. Place your pencil inside the tin can with the eraser side up (the pencil will need to be just tall enough to stand inside the tin can). Find the center of the straw and push a straight pin through it and into the pencil eraser. Make sure that it's not too tightly secured; the straw will need to be able to swing as the wind blows. Mark the sides of the can with N, S, E and W. Attach the tin can to a flat board with modeling clay and wait for the wind to blow! The arrow will point in the direction the wind is blowing from.

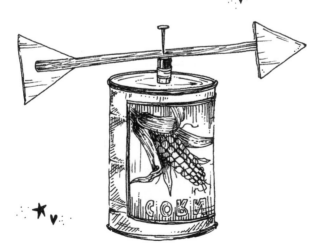

Did you know that each month the full moon has a special name? It's known as the Strawberry Moon in June, Thunder Moon in July, and Green Corn Moon in August.

Time for the
End·of·Summer
Gathering
AT THE
lake

Gathering at the Lake

Cornmeal Fried Catfish & Fresh Tartar Sauce

Very easy to prepare!

3 catfish fillets
1/2 c. golden mustard
1 c. cornmeal

1 t. salt
1/2 t. pepper
2 T. oil

Rinse and dry fillets then brush with mustard. Combine cornmeal, salt and pepper into a large zipping bag, shake to mix well. Add fillets one at a time and shake to coat. Add oil to skillet and fry fillet until golden. Place fillet in a brown paper bag to keep crisp and repeat with remaining fillets, adding oil as needed.

Fresh Tartar Sauce:

1/2 c. sour cream
1/2 c. mayonnaise
1 t. lemon juice

2 T. onion, diced
1 T. fresh parsley, chopped

Blend all ingredients thoroughly and place in a small bowl. Cover and refrigerate until cold. Yield 1-1/4 cups.

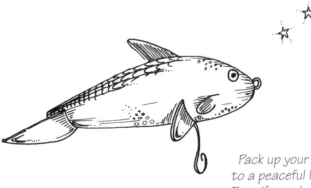

Pack up your fishing gear and head to a peaceful lake or shady riverbank. Even if you don't catch any fish, you'll enjoy a day of relaxing fun!

Hushpuppies

Nothing goes better with a fish dinner!

2 c. yellow cornmeal
1 T. flour
1 t. salt
1 t. baking powder
1/2 t. baking soda

3 T. white onion, chopped
1 c. buttermilk
1 egg, beaten
oil for frying

Combine cornmeal, flour, salt, baking powder and baking soda in a large mixing bowl. Blend in onion and buttermilk; mix well. Add egg and thoroughly combine. Pour enough oil into a deep fryer to equal 3 inches. Set deep fryer temperature to 375 degrees. Drop batter by tablespoonfuls into hot oil, turn and fry until golden. Drain on paper towels and repeat with remaining batter. Serves 4.

Pack your plates, flatware, cups and napkins in a fishing creel. A cricket box can double as a vase for wildflowers.

Gathering at the Lake

Corn Fritters

These can be made in a deep-fryer if you prefer.

1 egg
1/2 c. milk
12-oz. can corn
1 T. solid shortening, melted
1 c. flour

1 T. sugar
1/2 t. salt
1 t. baking powder
oil for frying

In a large mixing bowl, combine egg and milk. Blend in corn and shortening; mix well. In a separate bowl sift together flour, sugar, salt and baking powder. Slowly add to egg mixture and gently blend. Pour oil into skillet and drop batter by tablespoonfuls into a skillet. Fry until thoroughly cooked, about 5 minutes. Drain on paper towels and repeat. Makes approximately 20 fritters.

Use a fisherman's stool to hold desserts or baskets of apples. Create an easy tablecloth by covering your picnic table with newspaper and keep soda cool by icing them down in a clean minnow bucket.

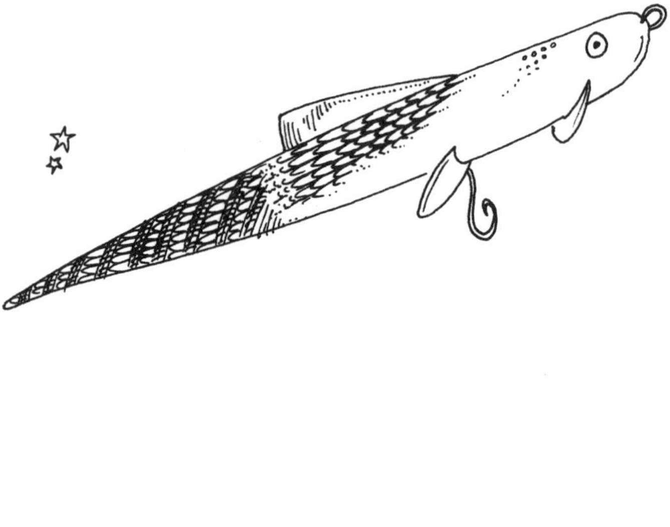

Garden Vegetable Jumble

A great way to use the last veggies from this year's garden.

2 T. oil
4 c. zucchini, chopped
1 c. onion, chopped
1 c. carrots, chopped
1 green pepper, sliced into strips

2 t. fresh basil, diced
1 tomato, chopped
salt and pepper to taste
1/2 c. Cheddar cheese, shredded

Place oil in a skillet, turning to coat bottom. Add zucchini, onions, carrots, green pepper and cook over medium heat until crisp-tender. Add basil and tomato, stirring to mix. Salt and pepper, add cheese on top. Cover skillet and allow cheese to melt.

Have fun with a rustic outdoor tablesetting. A centerpiece of pinecones, bird-houses, autumn leaves, berries and tree limbs are perfect for a dinner at the lake! Add some lanterns, baskets and serve drinks in canning jars. Slingshots make fun napkin rings!

Gathering at the Lake

Lakeside Bean Soup

Prepare part of this hearty soup the night before and you can finish cooking it over your campfire!

1-1/2 c. dried navy beans
1/4 lb. bacon, cut into 1" slices
2 T. oil
1 onion, chopped
2 c. carrots, sliced
2 tomatoes, chopped
1 t. thyme
1 t. oregano
2 c. elbow macaroni
Garnish: parsley, grated
    Parmesan cheese

Place beans in a Dutch oven; cover with water and let soak overnight. Rinse beans and cover with fresh water. Add bacon, simmer covered for 2 hours. In a skillet, add oil and sauté onions and carrots until tender. Add tomatoes and herbs to bean mixture. Cook macaroni according to package directions, drain and add to bean mixture; simmer. Garnish with parsley and grated Parmesan as desired.

Sturdy cast iron skillets and Dutch ovens are perfect cookware for lakeside dinners.

Skillet Potato Pancakes

Crispy! You may want to garnish these with a dollop of sour cream and chives.

4 large baking potatoes	1 onion, diced
2 T. flour	1-1/2 t. salt
2 eggs	oil for frying

Wash potatoes, pat dry. Peel and grate in a large mixing bowl. Toss in flour and mix well. In a small bowl, beat together eggs, onion and salt. Pour over potatoes, mixing thoroughly. Heat cast iron skillet over coals or grill until medium-hot. Add 2 tablespoons of oil to the skillet, turning skillet to evenly distribute oil. Using a quarter-cup measure, drop potato mixture into hot skillet, spreading out slightly. Cook 2 minutes, or until crisp; turn and cook other side. Remove from heat and keep warm. Repeat with remaining potato mixture, adding oil to skillet as needed.

Purchase old pie tins at a yard sale...they make wonderful, inexpensive dinner plates!

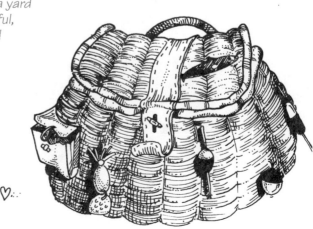

Gathering at the Lake

Brown Sugar Baked Beans

Cook these in a Dutch oven over the fire if you have time.

6 bacon slices
1 c. onion, chopped
2 28-oz. cans baked beans
2 15-oz. cans lima beans

1 c. barbecue sauce
3/4 c. brown sugar
2 T. yellow mustard

In a skillet, cook bacon until crispy; crumble and set aside. Sauté onions in bacon drippings until transparent. Combine onions, baked beans, lima beans, barbecue sauce, brown sugar and mustard; mix well. Pour into a baking dish, top with crumbled bacon. Bake at 350 degrees for one hour. Serves 10.

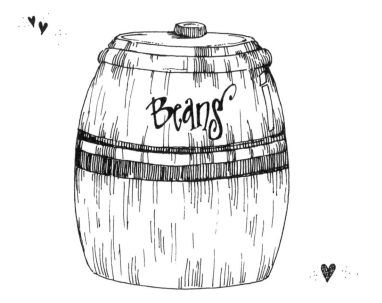

Help your children build an old-fashioned raft of boards.

Icebox Slaw

Make this when your garden is bursting with crisp cabbage, then savor it at the end of summer.

1 head cabbage, shredded
1 t. salt
2 carrots, peeled and grated
1 c. cider vinegar

1 c. sugar
1/4 c. fresh parsley, chopped
1/4 c. water

Mix cabbage and salt together in a large saucepan; cover and let sit one hour. Drain liquid from pan, add carrots. Combine vinegar, sugar, parsley and water in a large bowl, whisk until thoroughly blended. Pour over cabbage and toss. Place saucepan on medium heat and bring slaw mixture to a boil for one minute; remove from heat and cool. Place slaw in airtight containers or zipping bags and freeze. Will last up to 3 months in your freezer. Allow several hours for slaw to thaw before serving.

No time for a big camping trip? Sleep under the stars in your own backyard just for the night.

Mandarin-Romaine Salad

Crunchy and sweet...terrific with any meal.

1/2 c. sliced almonds
5 T. sugar, divided
1 T. water
1/2 head romaine lettuce,
   shredded
1/2 head iceberg lettuce,
   shredded
1 can mandarin oranges,
   drained

1 c. celery sliced
2 green onions, chopped
1/4 c. vegetable oil
2 T. cider vinegar
1/2 t. salt
dash of pepper
dash of hot pepper sauce
1 T. parsley flakes

Combine almonds, 3 tablespoons of sugar and water over low heat, stirring occasionally. Continue to cook until almonds are coated with sugar and appear dry; cool on a paper towel; set aside. In a large bowl, combine romaine and iceberg lettuces, oranges, celery and green onions; set aside while preparing dressing. In a medium mixing bowl, blend remaining ingredients and reserved sugar well. Before serving, toss with dressing mixture, add almonds and toss again.

Apple Dumplings & Cinnamon Ice Cream

An easy, old-fashioned dessert.

pastry for a double-crust pie
6 tart apples

1/3 c. sugar
2 T. half-and-half

Roll pastry into a rectangle approximately 18"x12", then cut into 5-inch squares. Peel and core apples, place one in the center of each pastry square. Blend sugar and half-and-half well, spoon into empty center of apple. Moisten edges of pastry with water. Pull up over apple, pinch to seal and twist slightly. Place dumplings on an ungreased baking pan and bake for 15 minutes at 400 degrees. Reduce heat to 350 degrees and bake an additional 30 minutes. Serves 6.

Cinnamon Ice Cream:

4 c. cream
3/4 c. sugar
1-1/2 t. vanilla
2 t. cinnamon

In a saucepan heat one cup of cream over low heat; do not boil. Mix in sugar, blending well until dissolved. Remove from heat, transfer to a mixing bowl and chill thoroughly. When completely chilled, add remaining cream, vanilla and cinnamon. Place in ice cream maker and follow manufacturer's directions for churning.

The end of summer brings new pleasures such as…hayrides, football games, fresh apple cider, pumpkin picking and no more weeding!

Choco-Scotch Treats

Quick and easy bar cookies that are perfect for snacking on.

1 c. sugar
1 c. light corn syrup
1 c. peanut butter

6 c. crispy rice cereal
1 c. butterscotch chips
1 c. chocolate chips

In a 3-quart saucepan, combine sugar and corn syrup. Cook over medium heat, stirring frequently until mixture begins to bubble; remove from heat. Blend in peanut butter, mixing well. Add cereal and stir. Press into a well-buttered 13"x9" baking dish. Melt butterscotch and chocolate chips in a double boiler; spread over cereal mixture. Cool until firm and cut into bars.

Make a cornhusk wreath! Remove the husks from dried ears of corn and fold them in half. Wrap ends with thin wire and then place them on a straw wreath, covering all sides. Add dried yarrow, bittersweet and wheat for a wonderful end-of-summer decoration!

Lavender Lemonade

Steal away to a quiet spot and savor a glass of this lemonade.

12-oz. can frozen lemonade
   concentrate
1 gal. cold water
1/4 c. dried lavender blossoms

2 c. boiling water
Garnish: mint or lemon balm
   sprigs

Combine the frozen lemonade concentrate with cold water, mixing well. Steep lavender in boiling water for 10 minutes. Strain lavender blossoms from boiling water and discard. Combine remaining lavender concentrate with prepared lemonade. Chill well, garnish with a mint or lemon balm sprig. Serves 18.

Delight in the splendor of an early morning breakfast at the lake! The menu doesn't have to be fancy...fresh fruit, herb tea, homemade bread and butter. Enjoy the sunrise and birds singing to welcome the day!

Gathering at the Lake

Cinnamon Hot Chocolate

Evenings can be cool at summer's end, this will warm you up.

1/4 c. cocoa
1/4 c. sugar
1 c. boiling water

3 c. milk
6-inch cinnamon stick
1 t. vanilla

Using a double boiler, combine cocoa and sugar; slowly add in boiling water. Bring to a boil for 2 minutes, add milk and cinnamon stick. Heat for 10 minutes. Remove cinnamon stick and add vanilla, stir quickly to froth milk. Serves 4.

As sunset arrives at the lake, create floating apple candles. Scoop out the top of an apple, slip in a tea light and place candles in a glass bowl. Slowly add water and light the candles.

Enjoy the last warm days of summer...

by rounding up family and friends and heading to the lake! Begin with fresh fish cooked over an open fire and end the day with some cinnamon hot chocolate to warm you up as the evening chill creeps in.

Prepare the side dishes well in advance so you can concentrate on making the "big catch" and keeping the fire going. Soup and beans will stay warm in heavy crocks or a cast-iron Dutch oven. Hush puppies and corn fritters will keep toasty in a cloth-lined basket until dinner's ready.

Cans of soda or jugs of lemonade will be close at hand, as well as icy cold, when packed in large galvanized tubs filled with ice. Bring along some non-breakable blue spatterware, perfect for serving dinner on, and blue and white bandannas for large, lap-size napkins.

After some splashing in the lake and maybe a game of horseshoes, you'll really have worked up an appetite!

What a man needs in gardening is a
cast-iron back, with a hinge in it.
-Charles Dudley Warner

Harvest Sunflower Centerpiece

At the end of summer, when you're harvesting your flowers for fall arrangements or potpourri, save any sunflower heads you have left over for this casual harvest bouquet.

You'll need about 24 sunflowers, a block of florists' foam, 8"x4" clay pot, green moss, and several lengths of raffia approximately one yard long.

Choose and pick your sunflowers; set aside. Cut the florists' foam to fit snugly inside the clay pot; cover the surface with moss. Trim the stems of your sunflowers to about 4 inches and tuck into the foam block, filling in any empty areas with smaller sunflowers if needed. Twist your raffia strands together and tie a bow around the upper rim of the clay pot.

Enjoy your end-of-summer sunflower bouquet, and within a few weeks it will dry and create a beautiful harvest centerpiece.

Have fun apple picking with your children! To help little ones reach up into the trees, cut a two-liter soda bottle in half around the middle. Tuck a broom stick into the spout and tape together. Just tap an apple gently and it should drop into the bottle scoop!

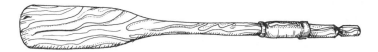

Hand-Painted Tins

Empty coffee cans can be turned into colorful water-proof carriers for utensils, napkins, or matches!

coffee can
spray primers
acrylic spray paint (blue and tan)
acrylic paints, for decorating

brushes
stencils
acrylic matte sealer

Rinse empty coffee cans; let dry. Following manufacturer's instructions, spray can with primer. To create an underwater look, spray the outside top two-thirds of the can blue; let dry. Paint the remaining bottom third with the tan spray paint, let both colors dry thoroughly.

Using the acrylic paints, stencil or free-hand colorful fish, crab, lobster, starfish and bubbles. Let the paints dry completely before spraying with a coat of sealer.

Old crates make perfect sideboards and trays for serving food lakeside. No need to worry if they get scratched or wet!

Gathering at the Lake

"Go Fish!" Napkins

Turn plain napkins into something fun!

tracing paper
graphite transfer paper
1/16-inch thick foam for crafting
4" square of wood
foam paint brush

non-toxic acrylic paints (yellow, orange, red, or green)
paper napkins, navy

Create a fun fish-shaped pattern on the tracing paper. Use transfer paper to transfer the pattern onto the crafting foam. Arrange the foam fish on the square of wood, and using a low-temperature hot glue gun press the fish in place.

For each napkin, use the foam brush to lightly coat the fish stamp with paint. Press the stamp onto the napkin and gently remove. Let dry thoroughly; repeat with remaining napkins.

Branches make clever curtain rods on a screened porch or summer cottage.

Trinket Fishing

While you're waiting for the "big catch," the kids can enjoy a game of Trinket Fishing. Before heading to the lake, pack a bag of fun, inexpensive trinkets...markers, squirt guns, stickers and costume jewelry are some ideas.

Tie a length of rope between 2 trees and lay a quilt over it. Remember to hang the quilt low enough for little ones, but not so low they can peek over. Using a fishing pole with a clothespin attached to the end of the line, let the kids take turns fishing for trinkets. An adult on the other side of the quilt can help the kids "catch" a trinket by clipping it to the clothespin.

Clean clay pots that have been lined with foil are terrific serving dishes for salads or chips.

Gathering at the Lake

Sunflower Feeder

As the summer comes to an end and autumn begins, the birds will be depending more on us for food. After you've enjoyed your sunflowers all summer long, it's time to turn them into charming birdfeeders for our feathered friends.

Gather dried sunflower heads, a variety of nuts, birdseed sticks (found at pet stores) and wheat stalks. Remove the stems from the sunflowers, then using spoonfuls of peanut butter, "glue" the nuts, birdseed sticks, or wheat onto the sunflower head. Set the sunflower head in an empty twig chair or on a garden bench...anywhere the birds can come to enjoy it.

The library has a variety of bird watching books available. Spend time with your children learning about the different types of birds that visit your own backyard!

Portable Flowerpot Candles

Extend your stay into the evening with a little candlelight.

small terra cotta pots   wooden skewers
adhesive clay   paraffin wax
wicks   wax crayons

Thoroughly wash and dry terra cotta pots. Plug the hole in each flowerpot bottom with adhesive clay. Measure the depth of your terra cotta pot, adding an extra inch. Tie one end of the wick onto a wooden skewer. Lay the skewer across the top of the terra cotta pot, centering the wick and gently pressing it into the clay.

Using a double boiler, melt paraffin wax over low heat. When melted, add crayon shavings for color. Carefully pour the melted wax into the terra cotta pot until it is two-thirds full. Allow the candle to cool completely, then trim the wick.

At the end of summer when the garden stops producing fresh flowers, you can still create pretty centerpieces. Fill a deep basket with several potted mums, fill a vase with dried hydrangeas or a crock with cattails and dried wheat. Grapevine baskets look great filled with ornamental kale and an old wooden bowl is beautiful overflowing with gourds, Indian corn and tiny pumpkins.

Index

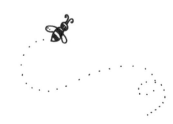

Index

watermelon 🍉 sunflowers 🌻 porch swing 🛋 fishing 🎣 fireflies ✨ crickets 🦗 homemade ice cream 🍦 croquet 🏑 barbecue 🍖 kids 👫 tomatoes 🍅 friends 😊 flowers 🌸 herbs 🌿 family 👪 lemonade 🍋 picnics 🧺 softball ⚾ family reunions 🎈 quilts 🧵 sweet corn 🌽

melon 🍉 sunflowers 🌻 porch swing 🛋 fishing 🎣

fireflies ✨ crickets 🦗 homemade ice cream 🍦 croquet 🏑 barbecue 🍖 kids 🧍

lemonade 🍋 picnics 🧺 softball ⚾ family reunions 🎉 quilts 🧵 sweet corn 🌽 water 🌽

tomatoes 🍅 family 🏠 flowers 🌸 herbs 🌿 friends 😊

Melon sunflowers porch swing fishing

Water sweet corn Quilts family reunions softball picnics lemonade

fireflies crickets homemade ice cream croquet barbecue kids

tomatoes family flowers herbs friends

watermelon 🍉 sunflowers 🌻 porch swing 🪑 fishing 🎣

fireflies ✨ crickets 🦗 homemade ice cream 🍦 croquet ⚙️ barbecue 🍺 kids

lemonade 🍋 picnics 🧺 softball ⚾ family reunions 🕊️ quilts 🧵 sweet corn 🌽 water

tomatoes 🍅 family 🏠 flowers 🌸 herbs 🌿 friends ☺️

watermelon · sunflowers · porch swing · fishing

fireflies

crickets

homemade ice cream

croquet

barbecue

kids

tomatoes · family · flowers · herbs · friends

lemonade · picnics · softball · family reunions · quilts · sweet corn

We've cooked up a whole collection of Gooseberry Patch® books!

Have a taste for more? Call us toll-free at

1-800-854-6673

We'll send you our latest catalog filled with snowmen, Santas, ornaments, candles, cookie cutters, gourmet goodies, salt-glazed pottery collectibles and MORE...including our best-selling cookbooks!

Phone us:
1·800·854·6673

Fax us:
1·740·363·7225

Visit our website:
www.gooseberrypatch.com

Send us your favorite recipe!

and the memory that makes it special for you!* We're putting together a brand new **Gooseberry Patch** cookbook, and you're invited to participate. If we select your recipe, your name will appear right along with it...and you'll receive a FREE copy of the book! Mail to:

Vickie & Jo Ann
Gooseberry Patch, Dept. BOOK
P.O. Box 190
Delaware, Ohio 43015

*Please help us by including the number of servings and all other necessary information!

watermelon 🍉 sunflowers 🌻 porch swing 🛋 fishing 🎣

fireflies ✨ crickets 🦗 homemade ice cream 🍦 croquet 🏏 barbecue 🍖 kids 🧒

tomatoes 🍅 family 👪 flowers 🌸 herbs 🌿 friends ☺

lemonade 🍋 picnics 🧺 softball ⚾ family reunions 💞 quilts 🧵 sweet corn 🌽